THE Wallace Rolls

OF

CHEROKEE FREEDMEN

IN

INDIAN TERRITORY

Relating to Cherokee Citizenship, 1881-1907

A Facsimile Reprinting

with an added

introduction & contents

Rolls Relating to Cherokee Citizenship, 1890-1896, also called **"Wallace Rolls,"**

Originally compiled by Wallace, John W. between 18
Department of the Interior. 1849- (Most Recent)

Indian Territory Division. ca. 1898-ca. 1907 (Predecessor)

Series: Revised Copies of the Wallace Rolls, ca. 1890 - ca. 1896
Record Group 75: Records of the Bureau of Indian Affairs, 1793 - 1999

This is a Preservation-Reproduction-Reference

Located in microfilm at the National Archives

at Washington, DC - Textual Reference (RDT1)

ISBN-13: 978-1544948928

ISBN-10: 1544948921

About this Book

Rolls Relating to Cherokee Citizenship, 1890-1896, also called **"Wallace Rolls,"** were compiled by John W. Wallace. The original rolls (registries) for the Authenticated, Admitted, and Rejected Freedmen, and the Free Negroes. Because of discrepancies, additional supplements were added. Individual entries give name, age, sex, residence, and other pertinent information. The individual rolls are generally arranged alphabetically by initial letter of surname of head of family, but occasionally they may first be divided into groups and districts. Each of the names are also issued an Office number, Wallace number and Cherokee number. There are also notes for many names, that they may be found on other rolls (registries).

The Cherokee Tribe challenged the citizenship status claims of several ex-slaves of the Cherokees of Indian Territory, and of some Shawnee and Delaware Indians claiming to be Cherokee citizens. The establishment of the freedmen's status was important in determining their right to live on Cherokee land and to share in annuity and other pay rolls. At various times during the 1890s, several Commissioners of Indian Affairs conducted investigations to compile Cherokee freedmen, Shawnee-Cherokee, and Delaware-Cherokee rolls.

These rolls were created because the Cherokee citizenship of many ex-slaves of the Cherokee in Indian Territory was disputed by the Cherokee tribe. The establishment of their status was important in determining their right to live on Cherokee land and to share in certain annuity and other payment, including a special $75,000 award voted by Congress on October 19, 1888. A series of investigations was conducted in order to compile the rolls of the Cherokee Freedmen. These investigations were conducted by John W. Wallace, 1889-1890; Leo E. Bennett, 1891-92; Marcus D. Shelby, 1893; James G. Dickson, 1895-96; and William Clifton, William Thompson, and Robert H. Kern, 1896-97.

This series contains rolls compiled by John W. Wallace, as a result of his investigations, and submitted with his final report, file 21833-90 of the series "Letters Received, 1881 - 1907" (ARC Identifier 300337). There are rolls for Authenticated, Admitted, and Rejected Freedmen; Free Negroes; Admitted and Rejected Shawnee and Delaware; and for special groups, mainly children and deceased persons.

For more info or assistance, it is recommended to visit:

https://www.archives.gov/research/native-americans

Contents

Schedule of names of Cherokee Freedmen made by John W. Wallace, Special Agent, appointed by the Secretary of the Interior, under a clause of the Indian Appropriation Act of March 2nd 1889 (25 Stats. p. 994) and under his instructions issued July 11. 1889, – as entitled to share with the Shawnees and Delawares in the per capita distribution of the sum of seventy-five thousand dollars ($75.000) appropriated by the Act of Congress approved October 19. 1888, (25 Stats. p. 609), and revised under the supervision of this Office.

Authenticated Freedmen

Office No	Dawes No	Chapter No	Names		age	sex	Residence	
1	1	1	Alberty	Jerry	57	M.	Convalescence Ditch	1 Clifton roll
2	2	2	"	Ruth	46	F	" "	2 "
3	3	4	"	Noah	22	M.	" "	4 "
4	4	5	"	Moses	20	M.	" "	5 "
5	5	6	"	John	18	M.	" "	"
6	6	7	"	Carrie	16	F	" "	6 "
7	7	8	"	Josh Jr.	14	M.	" "	7 "
8	8	9	"	Emma	12	F	" "	5 Emmy on Clifton Roll
9	9	10	"	Millie	11	F	" "	9
10	10		"	Sarah	9	F	" "	10 "
11	11		"	Fred	8	M.	" "	"
12	12		"	Bertha	7	F	" "	11 "
13	13	11	Alberty	Josh.	41	M.	" "	2394 Clifton roll
14	14		"	Castie daughter	6	F	" "	Born after Mar. 3. 1883 (14291) in 1884 14705 (915)
15	15	14	Adair	Robert	20	M.	" "	15 Clifton roll
16	16	15	"	William	25	M.	" "	16
17	17	476	Amstead	Lewis	36	M.	" "	51 "
18	18	478	"	Miss	28	F	" "	
19	19	16	Beck	William	20	M.	" "	1067 Clifton roll
20	20	17	"	Josie	32	F	" "	
21	21	18	Bird	Sophia	31	F	" "	
22	22	19	"	William	14	M.	" "	21 "
23	23	20	"	Henry	11	"	" "	19 "
24	24		"	Jesse	8	"	" "	
25	25		"	Anna	7	F	" "	

Authenticated Freedmen

Field No	Roller No	Church 4	Names		Age	Sex	Residence	
26	26	Ca Dit: 21	Brown	Abbie	40	F	Convee skonnia Dist	
27	27	22	Brown	Jesse	57	M.	" "	584 Clifton roll
28	28	23	"	Lucinda	38	F	" "	585 "
29	29	24	"	Sarah	23	F	" "	586 "
30	30	25	"	Anderson	20	M.	" "	587 "
31	31	26	"	Jesse Jr.	18	M.	" "	588 "
32	32	27	"	Willie	16	M.	" "	589 "
33	33	28	"	Polly	14	F	" "	590 "
34	34	29	"	L. B.	11	M.	" "	591 "
35	35		"	Becky	8	F	" "	592 "
36	36	30	Buffington	Mitt	35	M.	" "	Dau. of Eliza Rose 2469 Clifton roll
37	37	31	Burgess	Wm	37	M.	" "	33
38	38	32	"	Sarah	35	F	" "	34 "
39	39	33	"	Anderson Jane	16	M. F	" "	35 "
40	40	34	"	Maria	11	F	" "	36 "
41	41		"	Charlotte	9	F	" "	37 "
42	42			Charley	6	M.		Born Mar. 8. 1883 14705(91) 14291(91) 7031(91)
43	43	36	Brown	Israel	26	M.	" "	116 Clifton roll
44	44	37	Burgess	Minta	26	F	" "	
45	45	479	Boles	Susan	46	F	" "	yrs Clifton
46	46	483	Bondinot	Alexander	45	M.	" "	
47	47	484	Burgess	Wm	16	M.		

Authenticated Freedmen

Wich No.	Wallace No.	Chouteau No.	Names		Age	Sex	Residence	
48	48	Coodith 38	Chambers	Charles	55	M.	Coorueskonuee Dict.	✓ 11 Clifton rd
49	49	39	"	Caroline	38	F	" "	512 " "
50	50	40	"	John H.	28	M.	" "	Dul 94, See Vom 4 L E Bennett St 96
51	51	41	"	Eddie	12	M.	" "	573 Clifton
52	52	42	"	Mack	15	M.	" "	574 "
53	53		"	Emanuel	6	M.	" "	575 "
54	54	43	Carter	Riley	85	M.	" "	
55	55	44	Chouteau	Jip	69	M.	" "	Died 1891
56	56	45	"	Martha	55	F	" "	843 Clifton rd
57	57	47	Chouteau	John	28	M.	" "	153 Clifton rd
58	58	48	"	Sobe	27	M.	" "	106 "
59	59		"	Rosella	6	F		Born after Mar. 3, 1883 #1429(91) 7031(91)
60	60	49	Chouteau	Will	22	M.	" "	111 Clifton rd
61	61	50	"	Eli	20	M.	" "	792 Clifton rd
62	62	313	Coats	Sophimay Vann	30	F	"	Family Vann, Duplicate Same dd # 2296
63	63	57	Cordrey	Andy	29	M.	" "	122 Clifton rd
64	64		"	Mollie	7	F	" "	
65	65	485	Campbell	Charles	51	M.	" "	

Authenticated Freedmen

Office No.	Wallace No.	Sanford No.		Names	age	Sex	Residence	
66	66	Co.Dist 52	Dennis	Mary	31	F	Conocochronou Dist	535 Chf.61 Rae
67	67	53	"	Isabella	13	F	" "	536 " "
68	68	54	"	Bertha	11	F	" "	537 " "
69	69	55	"	Lama	10	F	" "	538 " "
70	70		"	Amanda	7	F	" "	539 " "
71	71	56	Daniels	Lewis D.	46	M.	" "	47
72	72	57	" "	Amanda	47	F	" "	49 " "
73	73	58	" "	Bettie	24	F	" "	50 " "
74	74	59	" "	Henry	23	M.	" "	Died 1891. See Ora 4 Pennell 3/91
75	75	60	" "	Jesse	13	M.	" "	48 Clifton roll
76	76	61	" "	Ruth	28	F	" "	17.6 Wife of Silas Kirk
77	77		Daniels	Ransom	50	M.	" "	2414 clifton roll
78	78	93	Foster	Edward	38	M.	" "	767 Clifton roll
79	79	97	"	Jennie	25	F	" "	194 Clifton roll Formerly French
80	80		"	Cora	8	F	" "	268 "
81	81	84	Foster	Randall	59	M.	" "	
82	82	85	"	Viney alias Mary	44	F	" "	152 Clifton roll
83	83	86	"	Thomas	23	M.	" "	153 "
84	84	87	"	Susan	19	F	" "	154 "
85	85	88	"	Peter alias Francis	17	M.	" "	
86	86	89	"	Martha alias Malinda	16	F	" "	155 "
87	87	90	"	Sarah	13	F	" "	156 "
88	88	91	"	Louisa alias Lucinda	11	F	" "	
89	89	92	"	Phillis	10	F	" "	157 "
90	90		"	Robert	7	M.	" "	

Authenticated Freedmen

Office No.	Wallace No.	Claiborne No.	Names		Age	Sex	Residence	
91	91	Cen Dist 74	Foster	Philip	38	M.	Connecticonnee Dist.	194 Clifton roll
92	92	75	"	Lou	36	F	" "	195 "
93	93		"	George H	6	M.	" "	252 "
94	94	71	Foster	Jerry	36	M.	" "	433 "
95	95	94	French	David	55	M.	" "	159 Clifton roll
96	96	95	"	Linda	50	F	" "	160 "
97	97	98	"	James alias Tom	22	M.	" "	163 "
98	98	99	"	Eli	19	M.	" "	162 "
99	99	72	Foster	Edna	34	F	" "	
100	100	79	Foster	Bexx Emma	26	F M.	" "	
101	101	96	French	Washington	31	M.	" "	161 "
102	102		"	Will	6	M.	" "	227 Born after Mar 3 '83 74291(91) Born March 14 '83-14705 7021(91)
103	103	70	Frye	Carrie (nee Drew)	25	F	" "	765 Clifton Formerly Drew
104	104	73	Foster	Melissa	56	F	" "	192 Clifton roll
105	105	80	"	Frances	25	F	" "	198 "
106	106	77	"	Lucinda	34	F	" "	197 "
107	107	83	"	Frank	14	M.	" "	209 "
108	108		"	Charles	9	M.	" "	
109	109		"	John	6	M.	" "	
110	110	78	"	Clara	33	F	" "	193 "
111	111		"	Maud	8	F	" "	
112	112		"	Jim	6	M.	" "	201 "
113	113	81	"	Jeff alias Josephine	22	F	" "	199 "
114	114	82	"	Dora	20	F	" "	

Authenticated Freedmen

File No.	Walker No.	Clarke No.	Names		Age	Sex	Residence	
'15	115	Con.Dist. 100	Grimmett	Ben	58	M.	Conaeskonwa Dist.	
'16	116	105	"	Elizabeth	18	F	"	"
'17	117	108	"	Melzie	13	F M.	"	"	290 Clifton roll
18	118	109	"	~~Samuel~~	10	F	"	"	Should be Squirel 12 W. See No 3(1)
'19	120	103	Grimmett	Henderson	26	M.	"	"	597 Clifton roll
20	121	"	"	Cora	7	F	"	"	598 "
'21	122	110	Glass	Robert	40	M.	"	"	478 "
'22	123	111	"	Lizzie	35	F	"	"	479 "
23	124	112	"	Abbie or Angeline	18	F	"	"	480 "
24	125	113	"	Randall	14	M.	"	"	481 "
'25	126	114	"	John	11	M.	"	"	482 "
'26	127	115	"	Lewis	10	M.	"	"	483 "
'27	128		"	Douglas	7	M.	"	"	484 "
'28	129	474	Grimmett	Easter	34	F	"	"	Same as 408. See 6/4291(91)
29	130		"	Nathan	13	M.	"	"	
30	131			~~Silvia~~	8	F	"	"	Same as 420. See 6/4291(91)
'31	132	118	Hammer	Emma G.	57	F	"	"	
32	133	68	Jackson	Mary	31	F	"	"	179 Clifton roll Family Drew
33	134	128	Kirk	Silas	32	M.	"	"	170 Clifton roll
34	135	486	Keyes	Charles	28	M.	"	"	398 "
35	136	222	"	Hannah	23	F	"	"	379 Family Alder
'36	137	127	Keyes	John	29	M.	"	"	392 Clifton roll

Authenticated Freedmen

Will No.	Roll No.	Voucher No. Cer. Dist.	Names		age	Sex	Residence	
137	138	134	Lasley	George W.	45	M.	Connecekonee Dist 244	Clifton roll
138	139	135	"	Jane	38	F	" " 245	"
139	140	136	"	Myra	19	F	" " 247	"
140	141	137	"	Lewis	16	M.	" " 246	"
141	142		"	Clara	7	F	" " 248	"
142	143	141	Landrum	John	48	M.	" " 437	"
143	144	142	"	Mary	41	F	" " 438	"
144	145	143	"	Major	26	M.	" " 439	"
145	146	144	"	Martha	24	F	" " Now wife of Chas. Hughs	
146	147	145	"	Polly	23	F	" " 441	
147	148	146	"	Andy	20	M.	" " 442	
148	149	147	"	Maria	16	F	" "	
149	150	148	"	Rhoda	13	F	" "	
150	151	149	"	Harry	12	M.	" " 443	
151	152	150	"	Nancy	11	F	" " 444	
152	153	446	Lowe	Julia	18	F	" " 24 Clifton roll Formerly Williams	
53	154	133	Leak	Albert	31	M.	" " 371 Clifton roll Dup. See # 2557	
54	155	129	Lowery	Harriet	34	F	" " See 402 & 403 clifton roll for children	
55	156	130	"	Fannie	16	F	" "	
56	157	131	"	Augustine	14	M.	" " 402 Clifton roll	
57	158	132	"	George	13	M.	" " 403 "	
58	159	151	Musgrove	Mary	60	F	" "	
59	160	152	"	Rider	21	M.	" " 202 Clifton roll	

Authenticated Freedmen

Heard No.	Wallace No.	Clayton No.	Names		age	Sex	Residence
160	161	Con Dist 153	Madden	Melinda	44	F	Convasskinva Dist 639 Clifton roll
'61	162	155	"	John	19	M.	" " 640 "
'62	163	156	"	Willie	13	M.	" " 641 "
'63	164	154	Rider	Sarah	21	F	" " 642 Formerly Madden
'64	165		Madden				Entered as No. 2125. Sec. 14291 (91)
'65	166		"				Entered as No. 2126. Sec. 14291 (91) Nos. 2125-2126 9. R. Bennett 1/91
66	167	157	Musgrove	George	55	M.	" " 812 Clifton roll
'67	168	158	"	Becky	50	F	" " 813 "
'68	169	160	"	Becky Ann	15	F	" " 815 "
'69	170	159	Musgrove	Wm	29	M.	" " 814 Clifton roll
170	171	Minnie 484	"	Judith	28	F	" " 517 Formerly Vann
171	172	Con Dist 165	McCoy	Cloe	110	F	" "
172	173	176	Markham	Willis	75	M.	" " 822 Clifton roll
173	174	180	"	Oswego	19	M.	" " 823 " "
174	175	182	Matthias	Sallie	49	F	" "
175	176	183	"	Angeline	18	F	" " 2440 Clifton roll
176	177	184	Miller	Tobe	21	M.	" "
177	178	185	Mosier	Hattie	18	F	" "
178	179	172	Markham	Fred	54	M.	" "
179	180	173	"	Julia	66	F	" "
180	181	174	"	Wm	25	M.	" " 736 Clifton roll
181	182	175	"	Sarah	20	F	" "

Authenticated Freedmen

Office No.	Roller No.	Cur Dist No.	Names		age	Sex	Residence	
182	183	166	Melton	Henry	55	M.	Cor was Skoonce Dist 575 Clifton	
183	184	157	"	Araminta	54	F	" "	580 "
184	185	169	"	Sallie	35	F	" .	Insane 552 Clifton
185	186	170	"	Stephen	17	M	" .	Insane 523 "
186	187	181	Melton	George	44	M.	. "	165 Clifton ave
187	188		"	Queen V	9	F	. .	168 "
188	189	190	Nave	Flora	30	F	" "	557 Clifton ave
189	190	189	Nave	Lewis	37	M.	" "	
190	191	191	Nave	Ellen	32	F	" "	2397 Clifton ave
191	192	192	"	Carrie or Cora	14	F	" "	500 Clifton ave
192	193	194	"	Ulyses jy Evans	10	M.	" "	2403 " "
193	194		"	George	8	M.	" "	2394 " "
194	195	480	Nelson	Jennie	28	F	" "	715 Clifton Formerly Bowls
195	196	278	Owens	Lizzie	23	F	" .	Formerly Ross At 41 Clifton ave
196	197	198	Orr	Thomas	40	M.	" .	
197	198	199	"	Margaret	60	F	" "	
198	199	200	Pack	Joe	35	M.	" .	671 Clifton

Authenticated Freedmen

		Con.Dist	Names		age	Sx	Residence	
199	200	444	Patterson	Frances	50	F.	Coowescoowee Dist	4 " Clifton roll
200	201	447	"	Ellen alias Alice	16	F.	" "	5 "
201	202	448	"	George	14	M.	" "	This family enrolled on
202	203	449	"	Amanda	11	F.	" "	Cherokee Roll as Williams
203	204		"	Minnie	8	F.	" "	
204	205	275	Ross	Frank	46	M.	" "	39 Clifton roll
205	206	277	"	Nathan	25	M.	" "	40 "
206	207	279	"	Matilda	20	F.	" "	42 "
207	208	280	"	Aggie	17	F.	" "	43 Clifton roll
208	209	281	"	Annie	13	F.	" "	44 "
209	210		"	Frank	9	M.	" "	45
210	211		"	Sylvester	8 months	M.	" "	Unknown to head of family #10291(92) Bennett says on P.R. # 204 don't know him
211	212	230	Ross	Sarah	70	F.	" "	Dead
212	213	210	Rogers	Rabb	55	M.	" "	686 Clifton
213	214	211	"	Nick	22	M.	" "	687 "
214	215	212	"	Jack	20	M.	" "	688 "
215	216	213	"	Henelin Jn	19	M.	" "	689 "
216	217	214	"	Clem Vicous	17	M.	" "	690 "
217	218	215	"	Jasper	14	M.	" "	691 "
218	219	216	"	Clara alias Andy	13	F.	" "	692 "
219	220	217	"	Rose	11	F.	" "	693 "
220	221		"	Lucy	8	F.	" "	694 "
221	222	274	Ragsdale	Frances	30	F.	" "	wife of John Johnson
222	223		"	Florence	9	F.	" "	
223	224		"	William	6	M.	" "	

Authenticated Freedmen

No.	Roll No.	Census No.	Names		age	Sex	Residence		
224	225	243	Rogers	Houston Sr.	49	M.	Cooweeskoowee Dist.	880	Clifton roll
225	226	244	"	Sidney	46	F	" "	881	
226	227	245	"	R. C.	21	M.	" "	882	
227	228	246	"	Mollie	20	F	" "		
228	229	247	"	Sam alias Suey	17	M.	" "		
229	230	248	"	Charles	15	M.	" "	883	
230	231	249	"	Eli	13	M.	" "	885	
231	232	250	"	Jack	10	M.	" "	886	
232	233	251	"	Lizzie	32	F	" "	845	
233	234		"	Anderson	7	M.	" "	887	
234	235	201	Rogers	Willis	40	M.	" "	344	"
235	236	202	"	Sarah	30	F	" "	345	
236	237	203	"	M. J.	17	F	" "	Died 1891, Born 4-3-91; Bennett
237	238	236	Rogers	Hero or Hig	38	M.	" "		
238	239	237	"	Esther	34	F	" "	742	Clifton roll
239	240	239	"	William	14	M.	" "	744	"
240	241	238	"	Pomp alias Tom	10	M.	" "	743	"
241	242		"	Betsey	7	F	" "	745	"
242	243	262	Rider	Jerry	32	M.	" "	774	Clifton roll
243	244	263	"	Ann	29	F	" "	775	"
244	245	264	"	Frank	12	M.	" "	830	"
245	246	265	"	Rube alias Lucy	10	M.	" "		"
246	247		"	Rose	8	F	" "	831	

Authenticated Freedmen

			Names		age	Sex	Residence	
247	248	266	Rider	James	45	M.	Convveskonvee Dist.	753 Clifton rad
248	249	269	"	Sam	19	M.	"	754 "
249	250	270	"	John	18	M.	"	755 "
250	251	271	"	Tom	15	M.	"	756 "
251	252	204	Rosey	Wig	35	M.	"	
252	253	205	"	Albert	11	M.	"	
253	254	206	Ross	Lizzie	40	F	"	137 "
254	255	208	"	Rachel	20	F	"	133 "
255	256	207	"	Thomas	17	M.	"	138 "
256	257	209	"	Samuel	15	M.	"	
257	258	219	Rider	Maria	52	F	"	397 "
258	259	220	"	Polly	37	F	"	363 "
259	260	224	"	Sallie	14	F	"	373 "
260	261	225	"	Maglin	12	M.	"	375 "
261	262	226	"	Charles	10	M.	"	374 "
262	263	228	Rogers	Helem V.	12	M.	"	
263	264	231	Rider	William	42	M.	"	808 Clifton rad
264	265	232	"	Eddie or Edie	30	F	"	809 Shmld te Edie 30. F see 7031 (91)
265	266	233	"	Bob	17	M.	"	810 "
266	267	235	"	Mary	12	F	"	811 "
267	268	240	Rogers	Lucy	110	F	"	
268	269	241	"	Lucinda	25	F	"	857

Authenticated Freedmen

Office No.	Gallery No.	Bureau No.	Names		Age	Sex	Residence	
269	270	253	Ross	Maria	39	F	Convasskuvve Dist	837 Clifton roll
270	271	254	"	Pntha	19	F	" "	838 " "
271	272	256	Rowe	Haywood	32	M	" "	854 Clifton roll
272	273	257	Ragsdale	Jonah	50	M	" "	658 Clifton
273	274	258	"	Annaca	36	F	" "	449 "
274	275	259	"	J.J.	19	M	" "	
275	276	260	Rider	Elijah	55	M	" "	772 Clifton roll
276	277	261	"	Lucy	60	F	" "	772 " "
277	278	272	Ross	George	38	M	" "	535 Clifton roll
278	279	487	Rogers	Reuben	15	M	" "	
279	280	488	"	Gabe	40	M	" "	
280	281	489	"	Susan	11	F	" "	
281	282	291	Sanders	Polly	65	F	" "	180 "
282	283	292	"	Ella	16	F	" "	
283	284	303	Sanders	G.M.	11	M	" "	
284	285	364	Smith	Melinda	27	F		
285	286	223	Scott	Jennie	18	F	" "	372 Clifton roll Formerly Rider
286	287		Still	Harry	38	M	" "	
287	288		"	Caledonia	13	M	" "	3168 Clifton roll

14

Authenticated Freedmen

(1864) No.	Wallace No.	Clarke No. Cro Dist	Names	age	Sex	Residence	
288	289	301	Saunders Ann	35	F	Convuskrove Dist.	2131 Clifton roll
289	290	302	" Minnie	19	F	" "	
290	291		" Eliza	8	F	" "	2132 " "
291	292	283	Saunders Daniel	46	M	" "	711 Clifton
292	293	284	" Melinda	43	F	" "	712 "
293	294	285	" Benjamin	20	M	" "	521 Clifton Roll
294	295	286	" Mary	19	F	" "	713
295	296	287	" Anna	15	F	" "	343 clyton roll
296	297	288	" Israel alias Joe	14	M	" "	
297	298	289	" Daniel Jr.	10	M	" "	714 Clifton roll
298	299	293	Saunders Reuben	37	M	" "	175 "
299	300	294	" Alice	34	F	" "	176 "
300	301	295	" Lillie	20	F	" "	
301	302	296	" Rose	18	F	" "	
302	303	297	" Mike	14	M	" "	
303	304	298	" George	12	M	" "	Died 1891 Born 4 79, Barnett
304	305	299	" Dennis B.	10	M	" "	" " "
305	306		" Alice C.	8	F	" "	
306	307	360	Saunders Lewis	29	M	" "	1339 Clifton roll
307	308	102	Starr Georgie	28	F	" "	230 Clifton roll formerly Grimmett

Authenticated Freedmen

Wise #	Tolbert #	Drennen #		Names	age	Sex	Residence	
368	309	Co Dist 306	Taylor	Nancy	55	F	Cornerstone Dist	217 Clifton roll
309	310	307	"	Patsey	26	F	" "	221 "
310	311	308	"	Henry	20	M.	" "	220 "
311	312	309	"	Mary	19	F	" "	219 "
312	313	311	"	Sissie	10	F	" "	Died 1871
313	314		"	Maggie	9	F	" "	218 "
314	315	490	Tyner	Nancy	31	F	" "	Dup. 1329 See 1349. Watts 1329 ?
315	316	349	Vann	Polly	46	F	" "	143 Clifton roll
316	317	350	"	Eli	14	M.	" "	144 "
317	318	351	"	Joseph alias Josh	12	M.	" "	145 "
318	319	352	"	Lewis	10	M.	" "	146 "
319	320	330	Vann	Eli	35	M.	" "	362 "
320	321	332	"	Vic	19	F	" "	364 "
321	322	383	"	Lizzie	14	F	" "	366 "
322	323	334	"	David	16	M.	" "	365 "
323	324	335	"	Lulu alias Laura	12	F	" "	367 "
324	325		"	Laura	7	F	" "	368 "
325	326	367	Vann	James	32	M.	" "	
326	327	368	"	Rosie	31	F	" "	
327	328	369	"	Ben	33	M.	" "	Ree 707 Clifton roll
328	329		"	Frije	8	F	" "	
329	330	385	Vann	Wm	30	M.	" "	500 Clifton Roll
330	331	386	"	Sarah	31	F	" "	501 " "
331	332	387	"	Tildy	11	F	" "	

Authenticated Freedmen

Hler No	Dollea No	Chapman No	Names		age	Sex	Residence	
332	333	324	Vann	Gilbat	35	M.	Conneskoowa Dist. 309 Clifton roll	
333	334	491	Vann	John	46	M.	" "	
334	335	492	"	Sarah	35	F	" "	
335	336	493	"	George	15	M.	" " 475 Clifton roll	
336	337	494	"	Reed	11	M.	" "	
337	338	495	"	Joe	10	M.	" "	
338	339		"	Delilah	8	F	" "	
339	340	353	Vann	Edmond	46	M.	" " 50 Clifton roll	
340	341	354	"	Dinah	49	F	" " 502 Says she is 60	
341	342	355	"	Sarah	21	F	" " 504 Clif roll	
342	343	357	"	Willie	19	M.	" " Dead	
343	344	358	"	Eddie	17	M.	" " 505	
344	345	348	Vann	David	40	M.	" "	
345	346	315	Vann	Dank	38	M.	" " 61 Clifton roll	
346	347	316	"	Chick	38	F	" " 62	
347	348	317	"	Caroline	23	F	" Since reported to be dead	
348	349	319	"	Ellen	17	F	" " 63	
349	350	320	"	Ben	16	M.	" " 64	
350	351	321	"	Andy	11	M.	" "	
351	352		"	Elijah	8	M.	" "	

Authenticated Freedmen

Office №	Seller №	Cherokee №	Names		age	Sex	Residence		
		Co Dist							
352	353	342	Vann	Sam	59	M.	Cooweescoowee Dist	113	Clifton roll
353	354	343	"	Katie	49	F	" "	114	"
354	355	345	"	Amanda	18	F	" "	115	"
355	356	346	"	Willie	16	M.	" "	116	"
356	357	347	"	Rose	12	F	" "	117	"
357	358		"	Mary	8	F	" "	118	"
358	359	344	Vann	Joe	31	M.	" "		
359	360		"	Katie	7	F	" "	119	"
360	361	312	Vann	Stephen	30	M	" "	See to Vann Mar. 25, '93	"
361	362		"	Jim	11	M	" "	294	
362	363		"	Freddie	9	M.	" "		
363	364	392	Vann	Ben	32	M.	" "	See 737 Clifton roll	
364	365	326	Vann	Katie	55	F	" "		
365	366	329	"	Jane	22	F	" "		
366	367	336	Vann	Jesse	49	M	" "		
367	368	337	"	Cynthia	49	F	" "		
368	369	339	"	George	14	M	" "		
369	370	340	"	Cora	12	F	" "		
370	371	341	Vann	Jennie	45	F	" "		
371	372	360	Vann	Relda	40	F	" "		
372	373	361	"	Henry	20	M.	" "	791 Clifton roll	

Authenticated Freedmen

Office No.	Ballou No.	Charter No.	Names		Age	Sex	Residence	
373	374	362 Gro. Dist.	Vann	Jennie	35	F	Coweeskoowee Dist	
374	375	363	"	Sarah E	15	F	"	"
375	376	371	Vann	Mary	32	F	"	" 731 Clifton well
376	377	372	"	Tody or Tildy	17	M.	"	" 732 " "
377	378	373	"	Sam	15	M.	"	" 733 " "
378	379	374	"	Tillie or Lindsay	11	M.	"	" 734 " "
379	380	375	"	Julia	9	F	"	" 735 " "
380	381	388	Vann	Henry	21	M.	"	"
381	382	318	Vann	Lizzie	22	F	"	"
								Co. S Clifton well
382	383	378	Vann	Lena	27	F	"	" Now Crawford See case 1063–1067
383	384	379	" "	Johnson Jr.	25	M.	"	" 605 Clifton well
384	385	380	"	Cora	20	F	"	" 606 Now Markham See case 1063–1067
385	386	381	"	Upton	18	M.	"	" 607 Clifton
386	387	382	"	Henry	16	M.	"	" 608
387	388	384	"	Cunningham	10	M.	"	" 609
388	389	389	Vann	Sissie	22	F	"	"
389	390	390	"	William	17	M.	"	"
390	391	391	"	Eddie	15	M.	"	"
391	392	322	Vann	George W.	40	M.	"	" 2205 "
392	393	592 Ill. Dist.	Vann	Ben	55	M.	"	"
393	394	593 Ill. Dist.	"	Grace	50	F	"	" 2615 "
394	395	594 Ill. Dist.	"	Albert	18	M.	"	"
395	396		Rowe	Charly	7	M.		

Authenticated Freedmen

Office No	Soldiers No	Teachers No Cor. Dist	Names	age	Sex	Residence	
396	397	3	White Louisa	24	F	Conveeskimee Dist Formerly Albaty	723 Clifton
397	398	422	Whitmire Eliza or Lizzie	55	F	" "	646 Clifton
398	399	423	" Thomas	21	M.	" "	647 "
399	400	430	Whitmire Mose Sr.	60	M.	" "	765½ Clifton
400	401	431	" Katie	50	F	" "	766½ "
401	402	432	" Dave	12	M.	" "	See No.3092 Dup. 5567
402	403	433	Whitmire Aaron	55	M.	" "	53 Clifton roll
403	404	434	" Ann	50	F	" "	54
404	405	438	" Walter alis Mattie	21	M.	" "	56
405	406	439	" Charles	19	M.	" "	2029b "
406	407	440	" Sarah	17	F	" "	55
407	408	441	Whitmire Rachel	35	F	" "	
408	409	442	" George or Georgia	12	M.	" "	
409	410	443	" Jack	10	M.	" "	
410	411	450	Wright Lucinda	80	F	" "	728 Clifton
411	412	456	" Isaac	27	M	" "	Dead
412	413	471	Wolf Abbie	24	F	" "	
413	414	472	" Nancy	20	F	" "	
414	415	460	Webber Rose	55	F	" "	747 Clifton roll
415	416	461	" John	19	M.	" "	
416	417	462	" Ellen	14	F	" "	751
417	418	473	Williams Bettie	27	F	" "	

Authenticated Freedmen

Office No.	Roller No.	Charlies No.	Names	age	Sex	Residence	
		Co. Dist					
418	419	474	Williams Hester alias Lucy	34	F	Coweeskoowee Dist.	Same as 28, see d 4291 (91)
419	420		" Alice	8	F	" "	"
420	421		" Sylvia	7	F	" "	Same as 130, see d 4291 (91)
421	422	412	Whitmire Dick	66	M	" "	346 Clifton
422	423	413	" Hannah	30	F	" "	
423	424	414	" Becky	17	F	" "	Dead
424	425	415	" Walter alias Mather	13	M	" "	347 "
425	426		" Charles	7	M	" "	349 "
426	427	417	Whitmire Dennis	40	M	" "	619 Clifton
427	428	418	" Lucy	35	F	" "	Says age is 16 (in 91) See 3071 (91)
428	429	419	" Joe	16	M	" "	See # 210420 (91) 477 Clifton
429	430		" Milissa	9	F	" "	
430		282	" Com	40	F	" "	Formerly "Still, Com"
431	431	403	Whitmire Minerva Mariah r.	36	F	" "	456 Clifton roll
432	432	406	" Susan	19	F	" "	458 "
433	433	407	" Bertha	17	F	" "	459 "
434	434	408	" Eliza	15	F	" "	460 "
435	435	409	" Gettie	13	M. F	" "	461 2nd payroll, See Vou. 5 4th Qur (91)
436	436	410	" Minnie	12	F	" "	
437	437	411	" Willie	10	M	" "	462 "
438	438	395	Whitmire Nathan	28	M	" "	625 Clifton
439	439	405	Whitmire Segal	24	M	" "	457 "
440	440	475	Williams Alfred	14 22	M	" "	244 Clifton roll
441	441	168	Ward Nancy	23	F	" "	581 Clifton Formerly Melton

Authenticated Freedmen

Office No	Village No	Cluster No Credit	Names		age	Sex	Residence	
442	442	457	Walker	Daniel	40	M	Conyeeshonna Dist.	849 Clifton roll
443	443	458	"	Aggie	28	F	" "	850 " "
444	444	459	"	Charlotte	11	F	" "	851 " "
445	445	424	Whitmire Dick Jr.		39	M	" "	200 " "
446	446	445	Washington Nancy		30	F	" "	23 Clifton roll Formerly Williams
447	447	393	Whitmire Lewis		48	M	" "	623 Clifton roll
448	448	394	"	Betsey	45	F	" "	624 "
449	449	396	"	Peggy	21	F	" "	626 "
450	450	397	"	Jesse James	19	M	" "	629 Should be James 20 M See 8031(??)
451	451	398	"	Jennie	18	F	" "	630 Clifton
452	452	399	"	Josie	15	F	" "	632
453	453	400	"	Willie	13	M F	" "	632 Should be Millie 14 F offid gr
454	454	401	"	Aaron Jr.	11	M	" "	634 Clifton
455	455		"	Alex	9	M	" "	635 "
456	456	425	Whitmire Betsey		70	F	" "	
457	457	426	"	Lomey	32	M	" "	652 Clifton roll
458	458	427	"	Mary	33	F	" "	653
459	459	428	"	Maggie	12	F	" "	654 " "
460	460	429	"	Josie	15	F	" "	655 " "
461	461		"	Isaac	10	M	" "	
462	462		"	William	7	M	" "	

Authenticated Freedmen

Office No.	Wallace No.	Clanton No.	Names		Age	Sex	Residence			
		Co. Dist.								
463	463	463	Webber	Samuel	44	M.	Coweescoowee Dist.	334	Clifton roll	
464	464	464	"	Sarah	34	F	" "	335	"
465	465	465	"	Nancy	21	F	" "		"
466	466	466	"	Lewis	19	M.	" "	3499	"
467	467	467	"	Aaron	16	M.	" "	336	"
468	468	468	"	Minerva	14	F	" "	333	"
469	469	470	"	David	11	M.	" "	339	"
470	470		"	Georgie Ann	8	F	" "	340	"
471	471		"	George Henry	8	M.	" "	341	"
		Can. Dist.							
472	472	1	Benge	Isaac	37	M.	Canadian Dist.	1786	"
473	473	2	"	Jennie	35	F	" "	1787	"
474	474	3	"	Charley	15	M.	" "	1788	"
475	475		"	Ned	9	M.	" "	1789	"
476	485	12	Drew	John	12	M.	" "	1916	"
477	486	13	"	Henry (Hannah)	11	M.	" "	1717 Should be Hannah's uncle See Bennetts Schedule #4	"
478	487	14	Drew	James	41	M.	" "	1757	Clifton roll
479	488		"	Wm.	17	M.	" "	1758	"
480	489		"	Lizzie	15	F	" "	1759	"
481	490		"	Cornelia	13	F	" "	1760	"
482	491		"	Talbert	11	M.	" "	1762	"
483	472		"	Amanda	9	F	" "	1761	"
484	493		"	Ida	7	F	" "		
485	494	21	Drew	Moses	28	M.	" "	493	Clifton roll
486	495	15	"	Will	14	M.	" "	1494	"
487	496	16	"	Mollie	14	F	" "		

Authenticated Freedmen

Office No.			Names		Age	Sex	Residence	
488	497	Can Dist 22	Drew	Ellen	24	F	Canadian Dist	1614 Clifton rope New Ellen Hant
489	498	20	Drew	James	28	M	" "	1578 Clifton roll
490	499		"	Mattie	8	F	" "	1579 "
491	502	26	Daniels	Sallie	24	F	" "	
492	503	27	Drew	Rachel	36	F	" "	1582 Clifton roll
493	504	42	Reed	Frank	10	M	" "	1483 "
494	505		Vann	Belle	8	F	" "	1484 "
495	506	32	Hicks	John or Jon.	40	M	" "	
496	507	31	Hawkins	Jerry	62	M	" "	
497	508	58	Johnson	Mary C.	24	F	" "	1218 Clifton roll formerly Sheppard
498	509	33	Latta	Allen	80	M	" "	
499	510	McDist 243	Landrum	Wm	28	M	" "	
500	511	McDist 244	"	Charity	28	F	" "	2702 Clifton roll
501	512	Can Dist 34	Mackey	Charles	55	M	" "	
502	513	37	"	Tony	28	M	" "	
503	514	36	"	Jennie	23	F	" "	1251 Clifton roll
504	515	35	"	Rufus	19	M	" "	1530 "
505	516	38	Nivens	Jordan	13	M	" "	
506	517	39	Rider	Jess	40	M	" "	1490 "
507	518	40	"	Red alias Bud	13	M	" "	1491 "

Authenticated Freedmen

Office No.	Williams No.	Winchester No.	Names		age	Sex	Residence	
508	520	Can. Dist. 44	Scales.	Lizzie	12	F	Canadian Dist	
509	521	55	Scales	Hannah	47	F	" "	
510	522	60	Starr	Rhoda	38	F	" "	
511	523	61	"	Viney	13	F	" "	
512	524	Ill. Dist. 439	Thomas	Hannah	33	F	" "	
513	525	Ill. Dist. 440	"	Lucy	19	F	" "	
514	526	Ill. Dist. 441	"	Emma	17	F	" "	age 14 on P.R.
515	527	Ill. Dist. 442	"	Wm.	12	M	" "	
516	528		"	Freddie	10	M	" "	
517	529	Ill. Dist. 100	Taylor	Fannie	26	F	" "	Formerly Cropo
518	530	Can. Dist. 65	Vann	Martin	75	M	" "	
519	531	69	Wright	Alice	29	F	" "	
520	532	70	"	Maggie	12	F	" "	1797 Clifton Doll
521	533	71	"	Charles	11	M	" "	1798 "
522	534	59	Williams	Edna	21	F	" "	Formerly Sheppard
523	535	72	Wolf	Susan	17	F	" "	
524	536	66	White	Fannie	40	F	" "	1345 Clifton ave
525	537	67	"	Lucinda	12	F	" "	1346
526	538	68	"	Nathan	11	M	" "	1347
527	2.000		"	Alice	7	F	" "	1348 "

Authenticated Freedmen

			Names		age	Sex	Residence	
528	539	1	Adair	Squire	70	M.	Delaware Dist.	
529	540	2	"	Eliza	39	F	" "	434 Clifton rell
530	541	3	Adams	Cora	30	F	" "	2386 Clifton Rell Now Cora Martin
531	542	5	"	Grace	15	F	" "	505 Clifton rell
532	543	6	"	Ada	13	F	" "	547 " "
533	544	7	"	Squire	11	M.	" "	548 " "
534	545	8	"	Emanuel alias Frank	10	M.	" "	2389
535	546	9	Blythe	Monroe	32	M.	" "	2254 Clifton rell
536	547	386	"	Martha	35	F	" "	Formerly Shaw
537	548	10	Bean	Lucinda	35	F		Disp. see #567 See #4291 (96)
538	549	11	Bean	Phillis	35	F	" "	500 Clifton Rell
539	550	56	Buffington	Alexander	35	M.	" "	
540	551	57	"	Ruth	34	F	" "	
541	552	58	"	James	13	M.	" "	
542	553	59	"	Wm	11	M.	" "	
543	554	60	Britton	Mary		F	" "	
544	555	61	"	William		M.	" "	
545	556	62	"	Caroline		F	" "	
546	557	63	"	Lottie A.		F	" "	
547	558	64	"	John		M.	" "	

Authenticated Freedmen

Office No.	Gallup No.	Chapman No.	Names		age	Sex	Residence	
		Del. Dist.						
548	560	65	Baldridge	Jack	33	M	Delaware Dist.	183 Clifton roll
549	561	66	"	Nancy	30	F	" "	184 "
550	562	67	"	Lavinia	11	F	" "	182 Clifton roll
551	563	68	"	Lucy	10	F	" "	185 "
552	564		"	Eliza	9	F	" "	186 "
553	565		"	Minnie	6	F		Born after Jul 3, 1883 (14291 91) 4 years old — Bennett's P Roll
554	566		"	Amanda	8	F	" "	187 Clifton roll Will be 10 June 91, born 4⅗, ⁄ 26
555	567	80	Buffington	John	29? 24	M	" "	99 Clifton roll
556	568	81	"	Ernest	20? 18	M	" "	241 "
557	569	75	Buffington	Gus	70	M	" "	239 Clifton
558	570	76	"	Mary	60	F	" "	240 "
559	571	79	"	Lucy	18 24	F	" "	97 Clifton roll wife of Henry Morgan
560	572	69	Bean	Lee		M	" "	
561	573	70	"	Alice		F	" "	See 568
562	574	71	"	Patsy		F	" "	See 569 See 567 P.R.
563	575	72	"	Ellen		F	" "	See 567
564	576	73	"	Pola		M	" "	
565	577	82	Brown	Margaret		F	" "	
566	578	83	Burrell	Franklin	30	M	" "	
567	579	(104) 85	Bean	Lucinda	35	F	" "	546 Clifton Roll Dup see 537. See 14291 (91)
568	580	84	"	Alice	18	F	" "	Dup see 2174. See 14291 (91)
569	581	86	"	Patsy	12	F	" "	
570	582	87	"	Hattie	19	F	" "	528 Clifton Roll
571	583	88	"	Eliza	12	F	" "	527 Clifton Roll

Authenticated Freedmen

Office No.	Dollar No.	Chapter No.	Names		age	Sex	Residence	
572	584	24 Del. Dist.	Beck	Mary J.	27	F	Delaware Dist.	Formerly Frye
573	585	36	Bean	Sallie	38	F	" "	In these 43 & Clifton role Formerly Martin
574	586		"	Carrie	8	F	" "	432 Clifton roll
575	587	110	Bean	Amy or Emma	35	F	" "	474 Clifton roll Formerly Martin
576	588	112	Martin	Hattie	17	F	" "	275 Clifton roll
577	589	113	"	Sallie	14	F	" "	276 " "
578	590	114	"	Lou	12	F	" "	277 " "
579	591		Davis	Maud	7	F	" "	278 " "
580	592	18	Chism	Rose	50	F	" "	404 " "
581	593	91	Cricket	Mary	65	F	" "	
582	594	63 Coo.Dist.	Downing	Lou	35	F	" "	469 Clifton roll
583	595	64 Coo.Dist.	"	Mary J.	14	F	" "	
584	596	65 Coo.Dist.	"	Amanda	13	F	" "	
585	597	66 Coo.Dist.	"	Thomas	11	M.	" "	
586	598		"	Susie	6	F	" "	
587	599	15 Del.Dist.	Downing	Zebedee	35	M.	" "	69 Clifton roll
588	600	16	"	Jennie	32	F	" "	70 "
589	601	17	"	Lavinia	13	F	" "	71 "
590	602	92	"	Henry	14	M.	" "	72 "
591	603	93	"	Walter	11	M.	" "	73 "
592	604		"	Manuel	7	M.	" "	74 "
593	605	18	Daugherty	Narcissa	44	F	" "	

Authenticated Freedmen

No.	No.	No.	Names		age	Sex	Residence	
594	606	Delaware Dist. 30	Davis	Fenity L	21	F	Delaware Dist	685 Clifton
595	607	Delaware Dist. 31	Daniels	Griffin	80	M.	" "	
596	608	Ill Dist 191	Foreman	Luelia	42	M.	" "	552 Clifton roll
597	609	Ill Dist 192	"	Flora	38	F	" "	553 "
598	610		"	Kittie	9	F	" "	554 "
599	611	Del Dist 21	Frye	Andrew	56	M.	" "	315 " "
600	612	22	"	Milly	51	F	" "	316 " "
601	613	94	"	Sarah	22	F	" "	Married "Isaac Rogers" admitted Ell 315
602	614	95	"	Susan alias Landy	20	F	" 321 Clifton roll "	319 Clifton roll 2nd single life, Sw brother 4th gener. 1891
603	615	96	"	Osmanda	18	M.	" "	Shoulder Landy 18 M. Sw 7031(91)
604	616	97	"	Viola	16	F	" "	322 Clifton roll
605	617	98	"	Ruth	14	F	" "	32 Clifton roll
606	618	99	"	Carrie	12	F	" "	323 "
607	619	100	"	Sophia Sophronia as	10	F	" "	324 "
608	620	26	Hardiman	Jennie	24	F	" "	551 Clifton roll
609	621	27	"	Joseph	20	M.	" "	554 " "
610	622	103	Landrum	Sam	21	M.	" "	Since reported dead
611	623	102	Landrum	Spence	35	M.	" "	700 Clifton
612	624		"	Albert	8	M.	" "	702
613	625	78	Ledman	Eliza	28	F	" "	Formerly Buffington 90
614	626		"	James	7	M.	" "	91 "

Authenticated Freedmen

Office No.	Southern No.	Cherokee No.		Names	age	Sex	Residence	
		2d Dist.						
615	627	30	Lynch	Tobias	35	M.	Delaware Dist.	495 Clifton roll
616	628	31	"	Joanna	24	F	" "	Not known head of family 14291
617	629		"	Myrtie	8	F	497 Clifton roll	Grand daughter of Winnie Ratcliffe 660 Does Bennett not mean 617?
618	630	101	Landrum	Winnie	55	F	" "	1154 Clifton roll.
619	631	28	Lynch	Allen	50	M	" .	329 Clifton roll
620	632	104	"	Cynthia	40	F	"	
621	633	106	"	Eddie	14	M	"	
622	634	107	"	Birdie	17	F	"	Drew as Cherokees in 1883 Sev 14291 (91) & 7031 (91)
623	635	108	"	Andrew	13	M	"	
624	636	109	"	Mary	11	F	"	
625	637	29	Lynch	Anderson	50	M	" "	255 Clifton roll
626	638		.	Ruth	31	F	" "	Formerly Mrs. Buffington
627	639		.	Rhoda	15	F	" "	
628	640		Buffington	Lucien	8	M.	" "	Child of 638 by former husband
629	641		Moore	Thomas	37	M.	" .	3359 Clifton roll
630	643	127	Morris	Sarah	23	F.	" .	730 Clifton roll Formerly Ratcliffe
631	644	111	Martin	Isaac	28	M.	" .	291 Clifton roll
632	..	105	Martin	Florence	21	F	" "	Formerly Lynch

Authenticated Freedmen.

No.	No.	No.	Names		Age	Sex	Residence	
633	645	115	Martin	Wilson	50	M	Delaware Dist.	271 Clifton roll
634	646	116	"	Patsy or Martha	44	F	" "	
635	647	118	"	Frank	19	M	" "	304 Clifton roll
636	648	119	"	Jerome James	16	M.	" "	
637	649	120	"	Mary	14	F	" "	307 "
638	650	121	"	Genl Blunt	13	M	" "	306 "
639	651	122	"	Nathaniel	14	M.	" "	723 Clifton roll Son of Silve Martin
640	652	37	Moore	Nelson	37	M	" "	671 Clifton roll
641	653	38	"	Rose	37	F	" "	672 "
642	654	123	"	Rhodus	17	M	" "	52 "
643	655	124	"	Emily F	15	F	" "	673 Clifton "
644	656	125	"	Charles or Chany	13	M.	" "	
645	657	126	"	Mary	10	F	" "	674 Clifton
646	658		"	Lewis	9	M.	" "	675 "
647	659	33	Martin	Juno	70	F		285 "
648	660	34	Mayfield	Elijah	60	M		
649	661	39	Rowe	Lewis	58	M.		77 Clifton roll
650	662	40	"	Chaney or Chana	55	F		78 "
651	663	41	"	Jesse	28	M		79 "
652	664	42	"	Eliza	27	F		80
653	665	43	"	Sophia	24	F		Now Brakebill
654	666	44	"	Laura	22	F		82 "
655	667	45	"	Martha A	19	F		83 "
656	668	90	Buffington	Florence	12	F		86 Daughter of Mary Jones wife of 665
657	669	49	Ratcliffe	Frank	25	M.		650 Clifton roll

Authenticated Freedmen

Office No.	Eastland No.	Southern No. Del Dist	Names		age	Sex	Residence	
658	670	128	Ratcliffe	Eda	26	F	Delaware Dist.	341 After roll
659	671	117	Ross	Ida	21	F	" "	2 & 70 clifton roll. Formerly Martin
666	672	47	Ratcliffe	Winnie	90	F	" "	
661	673		Stevenson	Andy		M	" "	
662	674		"	M. E.		M	" "	
663	675		"	Rosanna		F	" "	
664	676		"	M. A		F	" "	
665	677		"	J H		M	" "	
666	678		"	Fannie		F	" "	
667	679		Scales	Viney	51	F	" "	276 clifton roll
668	680		Thompson	Susan	29	F	" "	263 Formerly Martin
669	681		Martin	Joe	8	M	" "	264 "
670	682	131	Vann	Kate	26	F	" "	698 clifton "
671	683	52	Vann	Winter	44	F	" "	
672	684	51	Vann	Sam	28	M	" "	289 after Roll
673	685		"	Mary	8	F	" "	
674	686	55	Williams	Frances	30	F	" "	
675	687	132	"	Thursday	11	F	" "	
676	688	133	"	Eli	10	M	" "	

Authenticated Freedmen

Office No.	Brother No.	Cherokee No.	Names		age	sex	Residence		
677	689	Del Dist. 53	Williams	Arthur	54	M.	Delaware Dist.	411	Clifton roll
678	690	54	"	Eliza	30	F.	" "		
679	691		"	Arthur	10	M.	" "	412	"
680	692		"	Gus	9	M.	" "	413	"
681	693		"	Martha	7	F.	" "	414	"
682	694	G.S. Dist. 3	Alberty	Jeff	28	M.	Going Snake Dist.		
683	695	2	"	Jane	36	F.	" " "		
684	696	4	"	Maud	12	F.	" " "		Cherokee enroll her as Buffington
685	697		Grimmett	Ellis	40	M.	Oswego Kansas	3797	Clifton roll
686	698		"	Willie	22	M.	" "		
687	699		"	Bessie	14	F.	" "		
688	700		Lynch	Ellen	30	F.	Fort Reno. Act.	2789 Formerly Goldsby. Enrolled by Cherokee as "Buck"	Clifton roll
689	701		Goldsby	Georgia E. Crawford	15	F.	" " "	2790	Clifton "
690	702		Goldsby	Crawford alias	13	M.	" " "		
691	703		Goldsby	Clarence	12	M.	" " "	2792	Clifton roll
692	704		Goldsby	Luther	10	M.	" " "	2793	"
693	705	5	Taylor	Lewis	32	M.	Going Snake Dist.		
694	706	6	Weaver	Lewis	33	M.	" " "		

Authenticated Freedmen

Office No.	Wallace No.	Chambers No.	Names		age	Sex	Residence	
695	707		Alberty	Wm	38	M	Sequoyah Dist.	
696	708	Sequoyah 2	Benton	Amanda	50	F	" "	2285 clifton roll
697	709	3	"	Rizetta	21	F	" "	
698	710	4	"	Eddie	19	M	" "	2289 clifton roll
699	711	5	"	Samuel	17	M	" "	2290 " "
700	712	6	"	Willie	16	M	" "	2291 " "
701	713	7	"	Helen	11	F	" "	2292 " "
702	714		"	Isaiah	7	M	" "	2286 " "
703	715	79	Borden	Obbie	23	F	" "	2266 clifton roll. On Cherkee Roll as Ivy Miller wife of Oscar Borden
704	716	8	Benton	Cynthia	24	F	" "	2273 clifton roll
705	717	9	Barker	Billie	13	M	" "	2274 " " "
706	718		Barker	Harrison	8	M	" "	2275 " " "
707	719	10	Crossland	Isaac	37	M	" "	2298 clifton roll.
708	720	11	"	Elmira	34	F	" "	2299 " "
709	721	12	"	Sarah	12	F	" "	2300 " "
710	722		"	Henrietta	8	F	" "	
711	723		Cucumber	Sallie	70	F	" "	4446 " " Authenticated in Youngblood's list
712	724		Childers	Martha	33	F	" "	3171 clifton roll Now Reynolds
~~713~~	~~725~~		~~Obey for New Osceola~~		~~M~~		" "	Died before Mar. 3d 1883 4427 (91) Now deceased, not Youngblood
714	726		Campbell	Joe	27	M	" "	
715	727		"	Cynthia		F	" "	
716	728		"	Caroline		F	" "	2293 clifton roll Cherokee Caroline Charly

Authenticated Freedmen

Office No.	Dawes No.	Cherokee No. Seq Dist	Names		age	Sex	Residence	
717	729	14	Chukelate	Cynthia	35	F	Sequoyah Dist.	
718	730	13	"	Sam	15	M	" "	
719	731	15	"	Susan	90	F	" "	
720	732	16	Coody	Fannie	90	F	" "	
721	733	113	Childers	Richard	34	M	" "	
722	734	17	Depey	Tobbie	38	F	" "	2294 Clifton roll Cherokee roll "Tobbin" male
723	735	19	"	Jesse	15	M	" "	2295 " " Clifton roll Jessie female
724	736	20	Ellis	Bill	28	M	" "	776 Clifton roll
725	737	80	"	Rosetta	21	F	" "	777 formerly "Milton"
726	738	21	Eagle	Charles	39	M	" "	2213 Clifton roll
727	739	22	Foreman	Zack	40	M	"	2307 Clifton roll
728	740	23	"	Richard	39	M	" "	2350 " "
929	741	24	"	Sallie	24	F	" "	2351 " "
730	742	25	"	Ben	10	M	" "	2352 " "
731	743		"	Emma	8	F	" "	2353 " "
732	744		"	Jane	8	F	" "	2360 " "
	945	comes in after 758						
733	746		Foreman	Jerry	67	M	" "	1919 Clifton roll
734	747		"	Hannah	32	F	" "	1920 "
735	748		"	Allen	26	M	" "	2418 "
736	749		"	Lucinda	24	F	" "	
737	750		"	Maria	20	F	" "	
738	751		"	Solomon	18	M		Deaf
739	752		"	Benjamin	16	M	" "	

Authenticated Freedmen

6W... No	Wallace No	Shumate No Seg Dist	Names		Age	Sex	Residence	
740	753		Foreman	Harrison	39	M	Sequoyah Dist	2117 Clifton roll
741	754		"	Caroline	42	F	" "	2118 "
742	755		"	John	19	M	" "	1877 Clifton roll
743	756		"	Robert	17	M	" "	1879 "
744	757		"	Minnie	15	F	" "	2119 "
745	758		"	Foreman	9	M	" "	
746	746		"	Wynona	7	F	" "	Child of Lizzie Woodall paid to Lizzie Johnson
747	759	29	Hawk	Jack	36	M	"	
748	760	30	"	Mary	30	F	"	
749	761	31	"	Polly	12	F	"	
750	762	27	Holt	Peggy	14	F	"	
751	763	38	Johnson	Albert	31	M	"	2327 Clifton roll
752	764	33	Johnson	Julia	38	F	"	2214 Clifton roll
753	765	34	"	Lee	18	M	"	2215 "
754	766	35	"	Frank	16	M	"	2216 "
755	767	36	"	John	15	M	"	no Clifton roll
756	768	47	Johnson	Lewis	35	M	"	2278 Clifton roll
757	769	42	"	Mary	12	F	"	
758	770	43	"	Richard	10	M	"	Cherokee roll
759	771		"	James	9	M	"	2282 Clifton roll
760	772		"	Luella	7	F	"	2279 Clifton roll
761	773	54	Johnson	Aaron	56	M	"	1227 Clifton roll
762	774	59	"	Winlet	10	F	"	1229 "
763	775		"	Blanche	7	F	"	

Authenticated Freedmen

Official No.	Sullivan No.	Clifton No.	Names		Age	Sex	Residence		
764	776	56 Seq Dist	Johnson	Addie	24	F	Sequoyah Dist	1228 Clifton roll
765	777	57 444	Johnson	Ailsey	60	F	" "	
766	778	46	"	Dennis	28	M	" "	2427 Clifton roll
767	779		"	Dibbi	9	M	" "	2428 "
768	780	61	Jones	Eliza	52	F	" "	2316 Clifton roll
769	781	62	"	Jack	18	M	" "	2220 Clifton roll
770	782	63	"	Rilda	16	F	" "	2317 " "
771	783	64	"	Callis Jr.	16	M	" "	2318 " "
772	784	39	Johnson	Hannah	31	F	" "	772-773 not satisfactory identified by ... 2427 (6) ... Clifton roll 64 ... supposed to be same as 734-742
773	785	40	"	Cornelia	10	F	" "	who claims 773-785-40 as her son
774	786	45	Johnson	Nancy	55	F	" "	
775	787	66	Jones	Nancy	35	F	" "	2334 Clifton roll. Sees Caldwell
776	788	68	"	Eliza	18	F	" "	2343 Clifton roll
777	789	69	"	Andrew	15	M	" "	2345 " "
778	790	70	"	Sarah	14	F	" "	2346 " "
779	791	71	"	William	12	M	" "	2347 " "
780	792	72	"	Cornelius	12	M	" "	
781	793		"	Charles	9	M	" "	2536
782	794	114	Laflace	Bob	25	M	" "	1641 Clifton roll
783	795	65	Morris	Alice	29	F	" "	2369 Clifton roll
784	796	73	Milton	John	53	M	" "	2116 "

Authenticated Freedmen

Office No.	Dollard No.	Chester No.	Names		age	sex	Residence		
785	797	56	McEwen	George	32	M.	Sequoyah Dist		1/3 Apportia to the Cherokee by Blood
786	798	74	Milton	Nathan	53	M.	"	"	2258 clifton roll.
787	799	75	"	Rose	53	F	"	"	2259 " "
788	800	77	"	William	26	M	"	"	
789	801	81	"	Nathan Jr.	19	M	"	"	2256 clifton roll
790	802	82	"	Levi	18	M	"	"	790 Clifton roll
791	803	83	"	Mary	12	F	"	"	2260 " "
792	804	76	Milton	Susan	28	F	"	"	2261 clifton roll was Campbell
793	805	87	Mayfield	George	34	M	"	"	
794	806	88	McDaniel	Joanna	28	F	"	"	
795	807	67	Price	Ella	21	F	"	"	2339 clifton roll. formerly Jones
796	808	91	Riley	Louisa	30	F	"	"	2140 Clifton roll
797	809	89	Riley	Stephen	55	M.	"	"	
798	810	90	"	Emeline	56	F	"	"	
799	811	206 2nd Dist.	Gunter	Easter	70	F	"	"	
800	812	95 Seq. Dist.	Simons	Lot M.	14	M	"	"	
801	813	96	"	Linda	26	F	"	"	
802	814	97	Thompson	John	23	M.	"	"	114 Clifton roll

Authenticated Freedmen

Office No	Roll No	Census No	Names		Age	Sex	Residence	
803	815	Seq.Dist 99	Umpherson	Jerry	31	M	Sequoyah Dist.	2310 Clifton roll
804	816	100	"	Althea	29	F	" "	2311 "Cherkee" roll "Alice"
805	817	101	"	Joanna Frankie	10	Fe	" "	2312 Clifton roll
806	818		"	Susie	8	F	" "	2313 " "
807	819	102	Vann	Sallie	35	F	" "	
808	820	103	"	Nannie	33	F	" "	2443 Clifton roll
809	821	104	"	James	18	M	" "	2444 Clifton roll
810	822	m.Dist 596	Vann	Alexander	12	M	" "	
811	823	Seq.Dist 105	Vann	Jerry	35	M	" "	868 Clifton roll
812	824	112	Vann	Jno H (alButler)	31	M	See 2966 8(93) "	Dup. 3 1427 Same as No 1427 —
813	825	109	Wright	George	12	M	" "	Dup.3084, See 14291(91) Child of Ellie Wright
814	826		"	Thomas	8	M	" "	Son of Lewis Wright
815	827		"	Clifford	mo 8	M	See 2966 8(93) "	Son of Lewis Wright
816	828	110	Whitmire	James	32	M	" "	1574 Clifton roll
817	829	111	"	Mary	31	F	" "	1575 "
818	830	107	Whitmire	Jess	31	M	" "	2319 Clifton roll
819	831		"	Jim	8	M	" "	
820	832	26	Watson	Margaret	27	F	" "	2270 Clifton roll. Onnuely Gunter

Authenticated Freedmen

Office No	Dollar No	Cherokee No	Names		Age	Sex	Residence	
		Seq. Dist.						
821	833		Youngblood	Savina	44	F	Sequoyah Dist.	2142 Clifton roll
822	834		"	Reed Rhoda	21	M. F	" "	2143 Cherokee Certif. " "Ready"
823	835		"	Wynona	19	F	" "	" "
824	836		"	Ada or Ida	16	F	" "	Cherokee " "Alta"
825	837		"	Blanche	13	F	" "	2144 " "
826	838		"	Victoria	7	F	" "	2145 On certif " "Thelma"
		Saline Dist.						
827	839	1	Alberty	James	33	M	Saline Dist.	2409 Clifton roll
828	840	2	"	Rose	32	F	" "	767 Clifton roll
829	841	3	"	Martha	12	F	" "	768 "
830	842	4	"	Easter	16	F	" "	769 "
831	843	5	"	Lincoln	27	M.	" "	794 "
832	844		"	Jerry	6	M.	" "	770 "
833	845	8	Benter	Samuel	35	M.	" "	781 Clifton roll
834	846	9	"	Cynthia	32	F	" "	782 " "
835	847	10	"	Leroy	12	M.	" "	783 " "
836	848	11	"	Callie	11	F	" "	784 " "
837	849		"	Ella Jane	8	F	" "	785 " "
838	850	12	Blair	Squire	60	M		670 Clifton roll
839	851	13	"	Tony	35	M.		Cherokee roll "Sawney"
840	852	14	"	George	11	M.		Drew in 1883 as Cherokee # 1420 (91) 7081 (91)
841	853	15	Bean	Thizie or Eliza	90	F		396 Clifton roll
842	854	17	Bean	Rufus	22	M.		no 506 clifton
843	855	19	Bryant	Seney	16	M.		331 clifton
844	856	20	"	Rosetta	14	F		332 Cherokee roll "Rosetta"

Authenticated Freedmen

Office No.	Roll No.	Authen. No. Saline Dist.	Names		Ag	Sex	Residence	
845	857	21	Bean	Mahaly	35	F	Saline Dist.	dead
846	858	22	"	Joseph	19	M	" "	486 Clifton roll
847	859	23	"	Lewis	17	M	" "	466 "
848	860	24	"	John	13	M	" "	467 "
849	861	25	"	Mary	11	F	" "	468 "
850	862	26	"	Thomas	10	M	" "	469 "
851	863	27	"	Joshua	15	M	" "	470 "
852	864	28	Bean	Mary	15	F	" "	
853	865	111	Butler	J. B.	32	M	" "	
854	866	29	Blunt	Betsey	31	F	" "	On Cher. roll "Buffington"
855	867	108	Ward	Katie	12	F	" "	
856	868		Ware	Anica	9	F	" "	
857	869	35	Catron	Thomas	33	M	" "	507 Clifton roll
858	870	112	"	Lucy	12	F	" "	510 Clifton Roll two children Alph & Albert
859	871	36	"	Luney	11	M	" "	not satisfactorily identified 511 Clifton Roll
860	872	43	Fulsom	Sidney	33	F	" "	565 Clifton formerly Johnson
861	873	110	Freeman	Eliza	25	F	" "	Family Walker
862	874	49	Johnson	Cealy	27	F	" "	128 Clifton roll
863	875	71	Lynch	Lewis	33	M	" "	405 "
864	876	72	"	Abbie	45	F	" "	"Cher roll" "Ebby"
865	877	76	"	Evans	11	M	" "	407 "
866	878	77	"	Lula	10	F	" "	408 "

Authenticated Freedmen

		Saline Dist.	Names		age	Sex	Residence	
867	879	62	Lincoln		17	M	Saline Dist.	No other name
868	880	55	Lynch	Simon	59	M	" "	707 Clifton
869	881	56	"	Edey	46	F	" "	708 "
870	882	58	"	Wm	14	M	" "	418 "
871	883	59	"	Niuea	15	F	" "	475 "
872	884	60	"	Simon Jr.	13	M	" "	710 Clifton
873	885	63	Landrum	Giney	55	F	" "	
874	886	64	"	Oley	40	F	" "	
875	887	65	Landrum	George	68	M	" "	Dead
876	888	66	"	Caroline	50	F	" "	421 Clifton ville
877	889	68	Landrum Daniel		26	M	" "	
878	890	70	Landrum Wm L		22	M	" "	424 "
879	891	78	Lynch	Wm	72	M	" "	
880	892	79	"	Nellie	60	F	" "	
881	893	67	Landrum Samuel		28	M	" "	422 "
882	894	69	Landrum Sherman		23	M	" "	423 "
883	895	57	Lynch	Charlie	29	M	" "	709 Clifton
884	896		"	Eda	8	F	" "	
885	897	82	Murrell	Maggie	19	F	" "	351 "

Authenticated Freedmen

Office No.	Hollow No.	Chambers No.	Names		age	Sex	Residence	
		Saline Dist.						
886	898	80	Murrell	Sarah	50	F	Saline Dist.	350 Clifton roll
887	899	81	"	Jeffrey	21	M	" "	" "
888	900	83	"	Susan	16	F	" "	352 "
889	901	84	"	George	14	M	" "	353 "
890	902	85	"	Daisy	11	F	" "	354 "
891	903	51	McLain	Rachel	40	F	" "	512 Clifton Reg. formerly Johnson
892	904	52	Johnson	Jennie	21	F	" "	523 Clifton Roll
893	905	53	"	Malinda	16	F	" "	520 "
894	906	54	"	John	14	M	" "	510 Clifton? see 755
895	907	90	Rogers	Sam	30	M	" "	356 Clifton
896	908	91	Rogers	Allen	28	M	" "	355 Clifton
897	909	114	Rider	Emma	10	F	" "	
898	910	86	Richards	Eliza	26	F	" "	
899	911	93	Sutton	Sallie	13	F	" "	431 Clifton roll Child of Lewis Sutton Decd 2085
900	912	94	Thompson	Francis	18	F	" "	
901	913	95	"	Jordan	14	M	" "	567 Clifton Roll
902	914ª	109	Ward	Horace	34	M	" "	
		Ill. Dist.						
903	914b	1	Alberty	Edward	39	M	Illinois Dist Des 635 Clifton roll for child of
904	915	499	Alberty	Minta	29	F	" "	1368 Clifton roll formerly Vann

Authenticated Freedmen

Office No.	Soldier No.	Volunteer No. Ill Dist	Names		Age	Sex	Residence	
905	916	572	Adams	Synke	50	M	Illinois District	
906	917	573	"	Nancy	35	F	" "	
907	918	574	"	Lizzie	20	F	" "	4108 Clifton roll
908	919	6	Aldrich	Rachel	33	F	" "	1292 Clifton roll
909	920	7	"	Susan	16	F	" "	1293 "
910	921	8	"	Amos	12	M	" "	1295 "
911	922	9	"	James	10	M	" "	1294 "
912	923		"	Willie	7	M	" "	1296 "
913	924	11	Armstrong	Lydia	46	F	" "	1121 Clifton roll
914	925	33	Baker	Mary	21/19?	F	" "	Cherokee roll "May" Sphere
915	926		Drew	Tall	7?	M	" "	Child of 925. Investigate age & do not pay 915. unless born before march 2, 1885.
916	927	12	Blackburn	Edward	49	M	" "	
917	928	13	"	Willie	16	M	" "	
918	929	14	"	Frank	13	M	" "	
919	930	15	"	Sarah	11	F	" "	1005 Clifton roll
920	931		"	Chatie	9	F	" "	
921	932	17	Brewer	Seenie	50	F	" "	1038 Clifton roll
922	933	18	"	Jack	27	M	" "	Said to be in jail at Leavenworth

Authenticated Freedmen

Office No.	Pauper No.	Chereokee No. Ill Dist		Names	age	Sex	Residence	
923	934	34	Brown	Rev. Jack	62	M	Illinois Dist	
924	935	35	"	Katie	42	F	" "	1718 Clifton roll
925	936	37	"	Joseph	19	M	" "	1721 "
926	937	38	"	John	16	M	" "	1722 "
927	938	39	"	Annie	15	F	" "	1723 "
								1729
928	939	40	"	Delilah	12	F	" "	On Cherokee roll as 3 mos. in 1860
								1724 Clifton
929	940	41	"	Richard	10	M	" "	" " " 4 years in 1860
930	941		"	Fannie	7	F	" "	1719 Clifton roll
931	942	32	Brown	Hannah	66	F	" "	
932	943	48	Baldridge	Wheat	50	M	" "	1655 Clifton roll
933	944	49	"	Betsey	60	F	" "	
934	945		"	Ellen	9	F	" "	1656 "
935	946	42	Brewer	Ezekiel	66	M	" "	1658 "
936	947	43	"	Louisa	40	F	" "	1659 "
937	948	44	"	Samuel	18	M	" "	1660 "
938	949	45	"	Henry	16	M	" "	
939	950	46	"	David	15	M	" "	
940	951	47	"	Frances	11	F	" "	1907 "
941	952		"	Catherine	7	F	" "	1662 "
942	953	50	Baldridge	Peter	60	M	" "	1657 Clifton roll
943	954	52	Brown	William	45	M	" "	
944	955	54	Thomas	Mattie	23	F	" "	Formerly Brown
945	956	55	"	Jesse	16	M	" "	
6	957	56	Blackburn	Frank	20	M	" "	Dead

Authenticated Freedmen

Col No.	Wallace No.	Chambers No.	Names		age	sex	Residence	
947	958	Ill. Dist. 576	Buffington	Bud	29	M	Illinois Dist.	934 Clifton road
948	957		"	Jane	35	F	" "	
		"						
949	960	577	Beck	Demps	32	M	" "	
950	961	578	"	Alex	16	M	" "	1824 "
951	962	580	Beck	Angeline	40	F	" "	
952	963	581	Brooks	George	18	M	" "	
953	964		Beck	Harrison	20	M	" "	2765 Clifton road
954	965	563	"	Winnie	18	F	" "	1031 Clifton road Formerly Arntie
955	966	156	Brown	Sylvia	50	F	" "	155 Clifton road Formerly Fields 6
956	967		Beck	Lucy	40	F	" "	2764 Clifton road
957	968		"	Nathaniel	16	M	" "	2766 "
958	969		"	Jay	13	M	" "	2767 "
959	970		"	George	12	M	" "	2768 "
960	971		"	Joseph	8	M	" "	2769 "
961	972		"	Lewis	7	M	" "	2770 "
962	973		Brewer	Rabb.	26	M	" "	951 Clifton road
963	974	241	"	Sally	26	F	" "	Formerly Lowery
964	975		Butler	Mary	36	F	" "	2796 Clifton road Formerly Dann
965	976		"	Stella	16	F	" "	
	6							
966	977	292	Buffington	Melinda	19	F	" "	Formerly Nevens
967	978		Beck	William	21	M	" "	

Authenticated Freedmen

Office No	Wallace No	Wheeler No	Names		age	Sex	Residence	
968	979	Can Dist 4	Brown	Henry	42	M	Illinois Dist	1557 Clifton rall
969	980	5	"	Jane	38	F	" "	1558 "
970	981	6	"	William	19	M	" "	1557 "
971	982	7	"	Robert	17	M	" "	1561 "
972	983	8	"	Samuel	15	M	" "	1562 "
973	984	9	"	Fannie	13	F	" "	1563 "
974	985	"	"	Emma	9	F	" "	
975	986			George	7	M	" "	
976	987	57	Shephard	M. A.	67	F	" "	1217 Clifton rall
977	988	M Dist 437	Brady	Alice	20	F	" "	Formerly Thornton
978	989	438	Butler	Peggy	19	F	" "	Formerly Thornton
979	990	105	Crossland	Walter	22	M	" "	1664 Clifton rall
980	991	60	Crapo	Randall	27	M	" "	982 Clifton rall
981	992	410	"	Chaney	30	F	" "	Formerly Tucker
982	993	81	Crossland	Lewis	24	M	" "	452 Clifton rall
983	994	63	Chase	Maria	40	F	" "	929 Clifton rall
984	995	66	"	Julia	19	F	" "	929
985	996	67	"	Frank	13	M	" "	
986	997	68	"	Annie	11	F	" "	930 "
987	998	"	"	Ella	8	F	" "	
988	999	65	Chase	John	20	M	" "	2166
989	1000	Val. Dist 362	"	Ruth Ann	18	F	" "	Formerly Sheppard

Authenticated Freedmen

Office No.	Wallace No.	Charter No. III Dist.		Names	Age	Sex	Residence	
990	1001	64	✓ Chase	Mary	20	F	Illinois Dist.	109 Clifton roll from Buffington
991	1002	77	Crossland	George	56	M	" "	1508 Clifton roll
992	1003	78	"	Grace	45	F	" "	1509 "
993	1004	80	"	Jonah	25	M	" "	1510 1512
994	1005	82	Roach	Emma	19	F	" "	formerly Crossland
995	1006	83	Crossland	Morris	17	M	" "	1513
996	1007	84	"	Julia	14	F	" "	1514 "
997	1008	85	"	Henry	10	M	" "	1515 "
998	1009	79	Crossland	George Jr.	28	M	" "	
999	1010	86	Crapo	Alexander	36	M	" "	1074 Clifton roll
1000	1011	87	"	Thomas	12	M	" "	1075 "
1001	1012		"	Grace	7	F	" "	1076 "
1002	1013	88	Crapo	Joseph	32	M	" "	Residence unknown at present
1003	1014	92	Crapo	Lucy	32	F	" "	
1004	1015	95	Crapo	Jacob	52	M	" "	1714 Clifton roll residence 1315 & 16 Clifton roll
1005	1016	189	"	Judy	36	F	" "	formerly Foreman
1006	1017	98	"	Malinda	16	F	" "	1847 "
1007	1018	99	"	Susan	12	F	" "	1669 Clifton roll
1008	1019	178	Foreman	Benjamin	17	M	" "	1811 "
1009	1020	180	"	Cynthia	13	F	" "	1812 "
1010	1021	181	"	Wesley	11	M	" "	1813 "
1011	1022		"	Aaron	9	M	" "	1814 "
1012	1023	97	Crapo	Nellie	24	F	" "	1866 "

Authenticated Freedmen

Office No.	Wallace No.	Chastain No.	Names		Age	Sex	Residence	
1013	1024	103	Crossland	Andy	50	M	Illinois Dist.	
1014	1025	104	Crossland	Sally	64	F	" "	
1015	1026	106	Coody	Elijah	44	M	" "	1444 Clifton roll
1016	1027	107	"	Lydia	44	F	" "	1445 "
1017	1028	111	"	William	17	M	" "	
1018	1029	112	"	Betty	14	F	" "	
1019	1030	113	"	Sampson	11	M	" "	
1020	1031		"	Louvina	8	F	" "	
1021	1032	108	Coody	Alexander	22	M	" "	1441 Clifton roll
1022	1033	115	Choate	Josie	30	F	" "	1805 "
1023	1034	116	"	George	14	M	" "	1806 "
1024	1035	117	"	Minerva	13	F	" "	
1025	1036	118	"	Sam	18	M	" "	1807 "
1026	1037		"	Sherman	7	M	" "	1808 See 193 admitted
1027	1038	119	Crossland	Sam	29	M	" "	1416 Clifton roll
1028	1039		Pinder	Daniel	7	M	" "	
1029	1040	120	Carter	Lydia	21	F	" "	Dead
1030	1041	121	Davis	Emma	19	F	" "	1047 Clifton roll
1031	1042	123	Davis	Sarah	46	F	" "	145 Clifton
1032	1043	124	"	Rhoda	19	F	" "	944 Wife of Sherman Kirby

Authenticated Freedmen

Officer No.	Gallery No.	Volunteer No.	Names		Age	Sex	Residence	
1033	1044	Ill Dist 125	Davis	Abe	37	M	Illinois Dist	1122 Clifton rd
1034	1045	126	"	Fannie	29	F	" "	"
1035	1046	128	"	Caroline	11	F	" "	1125 "
1036	1047		"	William	8	M	" "	1124 "
1037	1048		"	Mary	7	F	" "	1126 "
1038	1049	134	Drew	George	38	M	" "	1778 "
1039	1050	135	"	Lottie	30	F	" "	1779 "
1040	1051	137	"	Lucy	13	F	" "	1780
1041	1052	139	Drew	Joshua	36	M	" "	1666 "
1042	1053	140	"	Rose	30	F	" "	
1043	1054	141	"	Sally	13	F	" "	1667 "
1044	1055	142	"	Jennie	11	F	" "	1668 "
1045	1056		"	Isaac	8	M	" "	
1046	1057	138	Dick	Blnsnv	10	M	" "	
1047	1058	Can Dist 19	Drew	Thomas	32	M	" "	1748
1048	1059	Ill Dist 475	"	Ruth	29	F	" "	1749 formerly Vann
1049	1060	Can Dist 25	"	Benjamin	12	M	" "	1488 Clifton rd
1050	1061	Ill Dist 582	Eaton	Jane	58	F	" "	1489 "
1051	1062	173	Field	Abraham	39	M	" "	1741 "
1052	1063	174	"	Sally	28	F	" "	1742 "
1053	1064		"	Diana	7	F	" "	1743 "

Authenticated Freedmen

Office No	Dawson No	Cherokee No		Names	age	Sex	Residence	
		Ill Dist						
1054	1065	161	Fields	John	75	M	Illinois Dist	Dead
1055	1066	162	"	Mary	55	F	" "	1776 Clifton roll
1056	1067		"	Emma	8	F	" "	1777 "
1057	1068	163	Fields	Michael	57	M	" "	1007 Clifton roll
1058	1069	164	"	Omie	48	F	" "	1008 "
1059	1070	165	"	William	31	M	" "	1009 "
1060	1071	274	Mackey	Amanda	18	F	" "	1610 "
1061	1072	166	Fields	Rockwell	60	M	" "	1706 "
1062	1073	167	"	Lydia	48	F	" "	1707 "
1063	1074	168	"	George Ann	18	F	" "	1708 On Cherokee roll "Sarah"
1064	1075	169	"	Fannie	16	F	" "	1710
1065	1076	170	"	Maggie	13	F	" "	1709
1066	1077	171	"	James	11	M	" "	1711
1067	1078	172	"	Lulah	10	F	" "	1712
1068	1079		"	Sarah	7	F	" "	
1069	1080	182	Fish	Hannie	28	F	" "	
1070	1681	183	"	Reader	10	M	" "	
1071	1082	152	Foreman	Caroline	54	F	" "	937 Clifton roll
1072	1083	155	"	Indich	23	F	" "	989 "
1073	1084	156	"	Annie	16	F	" "	
1074	1085	157	"	Fannie	14	F	" "	970 "
1075	1086	165	Foreman	Delilah	44	F	" "	
1076	1087	187	"	Abraham	21	M	" "	1548 "
1077	1088	188	"	James	14	M	" "	1773 "
1078	1089		"	Carrie	9	F	" "	

Authenticated Freedmen

Office No.	Wallace No.	Clifton No.	Names		age	Sex	Residence	
		Ill. Dist.						
1079	1090	186	Foreman	Jacob	37	M	Illinois Dist.	1764 Clifton roll
1080	1091	526	"	Leah	27	F	" "	1765 Formerly Vann
1081	1092	176	Foreman	Mary	38	F	" "	185~ Clifton Cherokee roll, age yrs ago 15 in 1880
1082	1093	190	Foreman	Jesse	31	M	" "	1879 Clifton roll
1083	1094	193	Foster	Amanda	60	F	" "	924 Clifton roll
1084	1095	195	George	Arch	45	M	" "	
1085	1096	196	"	Willie	19	M	" "	
1086	1097	197	"	Stephen	17	M	" "	
1087	1098	202	Glass	John	32	M	" "	
1088	1099	203	"	Inkey	63	M	" "	
1089	1100	204	"	Ned or Neil	13	M	" "	1626 Clifton roll
1090	1101	311	"	Sarah	22	F	" "	1625 Clifton roll Formerly Payne
1091	1102	198	Glass	Philip	40	M	" "	1612 Clifton roll On Cherokee Roll "Isaac"
1092	1103	200	"	Samuel	19	M	" "	1613 Clifton roll
1093	1104	201	"	Mary	15	F	" "	
		Can.Dist.						
1094	1105	28	Glass	Fox	47	M	" "	1617 "
1095	1106	29	"	Lucy	39	F	" "	1618 "
1096	1107	30	"	Minerva	16	F	" "	1619 On Cher. roll "" "Mirena"
1097	1108		"	John	7	M	" "	1620 "
1098	1109	24	Drew	Henrietta	15	F	" "	1589 Clifton roll
1099	1110	23	"	Richard	21	M	" "	1828 "
		Ill. Dist.						
1100	1111	194	Gunter	Sukie	80	F	" "	

Authenticated Freedmen

Office No.	Roll No.	Chamber No.	Names		age	sex	Residence	
1101	1112	242 Convict man Dist.	Griffin	Biley	23	F	Illinois Dist.	Formerly Rogers
11 1102	1113	Ill. Dist. 3	Glandine	Alice	19	F	" "	Dis 12 40 Clifton roll Formerly Albany
1103	1114	207	Hudson	Peggy	39	F	" "	1317 Clifton roll
1104	1115	209	"	William	18	M	" "	
1105	1116	210	"	Frank	14	M	" "	1318 "
1106	1117	211	"	Mattie	12	F	" "	1319 "
1107	1118	212	"	Emma	11	F	" "	1320 "
1108	1119		"	Fannie	9	F	" "	1323 "
1109	1120	208	Hudson	Sarah	20	F	" "	1324 "
1110	1121		Nave	Killer	8	M	" "	McComm b/leaf family 14291 Sept 27 65
1111	1122	214	Haul	Louisa	38	F	" "	1588 Clifton roll
1112	1123	216	"	Lucinda	17	F	" "	On Cher. roll "Louisa Jr."
1113	1124	218	"	John	15	M	" "	
1114	1125	217	"	Josephine	14	F	" "	
1115	1126	219	Hudson	Susan	33	F	" "	2415 Clifton roll
1116	1127	220	"	Ellen	12	F	" "	2416 " "
1117	1128		"	Mattie	8	F	" "	
1118	1129	583	Holt	Alexander	33	M	" "	2031 Clifton roll
1119	1130	96	"	Lucy	37	F	" "	Formerly Craps
1120	1131	584	Johnson	Joseph	36	M	" "	949 Clifton roll

Office No.	Walker No.	Chandler No.	Names		ap	sex	Residence	
1121	1132	Job. Dist. 186	Johnson	Job	33	M	Illinois Dist	1134 Clifton roll
1122	1133	187	"	Charlotte	31	F	" "	" "
1123	1134	96	Dickson	Nathaniel	15	M	" "	1137 "
1124	1135		Johnson	Sam	9	M	" "	1135 "
1125	1136		"	Maggie	7	F	" "	1136 "
1126	1137	Ill Dist 93	Johnson	Peggy	28	F	" "	1869 Clifton roll Formerly Craps
1127	1138	Cam Dist 50	King	Mary	19	F	" "	1608 Clifton roll Formerly Snow
1128	1139	Joh Dist 230	Keys	Maria	30	F	" "	2034 Clifton roll Formerly Musgrove
1129	1140	231	Musgrove	Laura	12	F	" "	2036 Clifton roll
1130	1141	Ill Dist 585	Keys	Abraham	27	M	" "	1448 Clifton roll
1131	1142	586	Keys	Louisa	30	F	" "	1456 "
1132	1143	587	"	Henry	16	M	" "	1457 "
1133	1144	588	"	Ellen	14	F	" "	1458 "
1134	1145		"	Charles	7	M	" "	1459 "
1135	1146	589	Keys	Mary	21	F	" "	1463 "
1136	1147		"	Dora	8	F	" "	1464 "
1137	1148	230	Lewis	Jacob	35	M	" "	1689 1340 Clifton roll
1138	1149	269	"	Alice	22	F	" "	Formerly Mackey
1139	1150	232	"	Moses	9	M	" "	1688
1140	1151	242	Lovely	Charlotte	32	F	" "	

Authenticated Freedmen

Office No.	Wallace No.	Charter No.	Names		Age	Sex	Residence	
		Old Dist						
1141	1152	10	Lee	Lizzie	28	F	Illinois Dist.	On Cher. roll "Orig Adair"
1142	1153		"	Jimmie	8	M	" "	
1143	1154	248	Mayfield	Nellie	50	F	" "	1245 Clifton roll
1144	1155	250	"	Sallie	11	F	" "	1909 "
1145	1156	252	Mackey	Judith	80	F	" "	
1146	1157	266	"	Dennis	35	M	" "	1532 "
1147	1158	267	"	Nancy	55	F	" "	
1148	1159	268	"	Simon	13	M	" "	1533 "
1149	1160	253	Markham	Siz	27	M	" "	819 Clifton roll
1150	1161	254	Mackey	Roswell	69	M	" "	1361 "
1151	1162	255	"	Mary R.	44	F	" "	
1152	1163	257	"	Liamilia	25	F	" "	1363 "
1153	1164	258	"	Lizzie	23	F	" "	1364 "
1154	1165	262	"	Annie	14	F	" "	1440 "
1155	1166	263	"	Ellis	10	M	" "	1366 "
1156	1167	269	Mackey	Perry	45	M	" "	1651 "
1157	1168	270	"	Dinah	35	F	" "	1652 "
1158	1169	271	"	Mary	17	F	" "	1653 "
1159	1170	272	"	Perry Jr.	14	M	" "	1654 "
1160	1171	276	Mackey	Crockett	36	M	" "	1232 Clifton roll
1161	1172	287	"	Jane	35	F	" "	1046 Clifton roll formerly Crane
1162	1173	575	Berry	Charles	15	M	" "	
1163	1174	422	Duncan	Tilden	12	M	" "	
1164	1175		"	Ella	8	F		

Authenticated Freedmen

Office No.	Wallace No.	Calendar No.	Names		age	Sex	Residence	
1165	1176	Ill. Dist. 277	Mackey	Dan	35	M	Illinois Dist	1256 Clifton roll
1166	1177	279	"	Annie	12	F	"	"	"1256 On Cher. roll McKee
1167	1178	245	Monday	Katie	45	F	"	"	1424 Clifton roll formaly Landrum
1168	1179	246	Landrum	Joseph	24	M	"	"	1428 "
1169	1180	247	"	Curge	24	M	"	"	1427 On Cher. roll Carrie Landrum
1170	1181	256	Mackey	Ned	28	M	"	"	1362 Clifton roll
1171	1182	280	Mayfield	George	23	M	"	"	2472 Clifton roll
1172	1183	281	Mayfield	John	21	M	"	"	
1173	1184	283	McIntosh	Dias	25	M	"	"	1352 Clifton roll
1174	1185	285	Miller	Frank	20	M	"	"	1544 "
1175	1186		Mackey	Ellis	36	M	"	"	1590 "
1176	1187		"	Peggy	29	F	"	"	1591 Clifton roll
1177	1188		"	Katie	11	F	"	"	1592 "
1178	1189		"	George	9	M	"	"	1593
1179	1190		"	Baptiste	7	M	"	"	1594 "
1180	1191	Saline Dist. 113	Nave	Sarah	28	F	"	"	1692
1181	1192	Feh. Dist. 262	"	Lucy	12	F	"	"	1693 Only "Lucy" on Cher. roll
1182	1193	Feh. Dist. 246	Nave	Charles	56	M	"	"	2448 Clifton roll
1183	1194	257	"	Edward	17	M	"	"	2450 "
1184	1195	262	"	Lydia Ann	17	F	"	"	2451 "

Authenticated Freedmen

			Names		age	Sx	Residence	
1185	1196	Ill.Dist 245	Nivens	Rufus	23	M	Illinois Dist	1687 Clifton roll
1186	1197	Ill.Dist 289	Nivens	Isaac	50	M	" "	1098 Clifton roll
1187	1198	61	" "	Mary	40	F	" "	Formerly Carter
1188	1199	62	"	James	11	M	" "	On cher. roll as "James Carter"
1189	1200	293	"	Julia	16	F	" "	1021 Clifton roll
1190	1201	294	"	Sally	15	F	" "	1677 "
1191	1202	296	"	Charles	12	M	" "	
1192	1203		"	Henry	8	M	" "	1099 "
1193	1204	2	Nivens	Amanda	32	F	" "	1779 Formerly Albert
1194	1205	4	Albert	John	13	M	" "	1281 "
1195	1206	5	"	Cora	11	F	" "	1282 "
1196	1207	Ill.Dist 244	Nivens	Patsey	50	F	" "	1155 Clifton roll
1197	1208	49	Baker	Sallie	20	F	" "	1380 "
1198	1209	249	Nave	William	22	M	" "	668 Clifton roll
1199	1210	250	"	Cornelius	21	M	" "	1085 "
1200		Ill.Dist						
1200	1211	297	Payne	Rachel	55	F	" "	
1201	1212	403	Thomas	Florence	17	F	" "	
1202	1213	404	Tyner	Rhoda	13	F	" "	1368 Clifton roll
1203	1214		Walker	Clark	9	M	" "	
1204	1215	304	Jack	Dora	16	F	" "	1912 Dup. see # 2713
1205	1216	305	Parks	Bass	66	M	" "	1143 Clifton roll
1206	1217	306	"	Nellie	45	F	" "	1144 " "

Authenticated Freedmen

Office No.	Wallace No.	Number No.	Names		age	Sex	Residence	
1207	1218	Ill. Dist. 307	Parks	Mack	28	M	Illinois Dist.	1145 Clifton roll
1208	1219	Sequoyah 98	"	Laura	20	F	" "	1147 Formerly "Thompson"
1209	1220	Ill. Dist. 309	Payne	Wallace	60	M	" "	2705 Clifton roll Age on Cher. roll of 1880 - 40 yrs
1210	1221	458	"	Rose	33	F	" "	Formerly Vann
1211	1222	310	Payne	Jackson	24	M	" "	1582 Clifton roll
1212	1223	Coline Dist. 6	"	Ruth	22	F	" "	Formerly Albery (Insane)
1213	1224	Ill. Dist. 215	Price	Emma	21	F	" "	72435 Clifton roll Formerly Hanes
1214	1225	19	Porter	Nannie	21	F	" "	1057 Clifton roll Formerly Brewer
1215	1226	350	Riley	Robin	33	M	" "	1725 Clifton roll On Cher. roll as Adam
1216	1227	102	"	Emma	25	F	" "	1726 Formerly Crapo
1217	1228	352	Riley	Solomon	34	M	" "	1730 Clifton roll
1218	1229	353	"	Lucinda	32	F	" "	1731 "
1219	1230	354	"	Lewis	16	M	" "	1732 "
1220	1231	355	"	Jefferson	10	M	" "	1733 "
1221	1232	500	Reynolds	Nancy	24	F	" "	1247 Clifton roll Formerly Vann
1222	1233	330	Roach	Daniel	67	M	" "	1853 Clifton
1223	1234	336	"	Samuel	13	M	" "	1858 Clifton roll
1224	1235	337	"	Judith	14	F	" "	1857
1225	1236	338	"	Jesse	11	M	" "	1860
1226	1237	341	"	Susie	18	M	" "	750 Clifton roll
1227	1238	342	"	Carrie	16	F	" "	347
1228	1239	343	"	Bob	13	M	" "	760 "
1229	1240		"	Han	8	F	" "	1855
1230	1241		"	Lie	7	F		Not known to head of family

Authenticated Freedmen

			Names		ag	Sex	Residence	
1231	1242	Ill. Dist. 334	Roach	Nannie	18	F	Illinois Dist.	
1232	1243	340	Roach	Sarah	19	F	" "	1453 Clifton roll
1233	1244	333	Roach	Katie	19	F	" "	1442 Clifton roll
1234	1245	344	Roach	Joseph	33	M	" "	1460 Clifton roll
1235	1246	Convention List 69	"	Fannie	28	F	" "	1617 formerly Drew
1236	1247	Ill. Dist. 327	Roberson	Calvert	37	M	" "	1400 Clifton roll
1237	1248	Conven. Dist. 359	"	Malinda	24	F	" "	formerly Dann
1238	1249	Ill. Dist. 590	Roach	Jesse	79	M	" "	
1239	1250		"	Jennie	80	F	" "	on cher. certif. Jennie Rainwater
1240	1251	Conven. Dist. 221	Rider	Tony	29	M	" "	
1241	1252		"	Alice	7	F	" "	839 Clifton roll
1242	1253	Ill. Dist. 331	Roach	Rosa	40	F	" "	1854 "
1243	1254	332	Roach	Henry	23	M	" "	1539 "
1244	1255	335	"	Susan	17	F	" "	1856 "
1245	1256	323	Ross	George	96	M	" "	Dead

Authenticated Freedmen

Office No.	Wallace No.	Allen No.	Names		Age	Sex	Residence	
		Ill. Dist.						
1246	1257	315	Ross	Henry	42	M	Illinois Dist.	1273 Clifton roll
1247	1258	316	"	Polly	42	F	" "	1274 "
1248	1259	318	"	Ned	17	M	" "	1277 "
1249	1260	319	"	Willie	17	M	" "	
1250	1261	320	"	Alice	14	F	" "	1276 "
1251	1262	322	"	Maggie	12	F	" "	1279 "
1252	1263	317	Walker	Mary	19	F	" "	1275 "Formerly" Ross
1253	1264	324	Ross	Jesse	66	M	" "	Dead
1254	1265	325	"	Hannah	45	F	" "	
1255	1266	464	"	Edmond	17	M	" "	
1256	1267	326	"	Ruth	14	F	" "	999 Clifton roll
1257	1268	328	Roberson	Jemima	76	F	" "	927 Clifton roll On Cher. roll as 50 in 1880
1258	1269	413	Thompson	Bobbie	17	M	" "	On Cher. roll as "Bob Thompson
1259	1270	415	"	Joseph	15	M	" "	
1260	1271	531	Vann	Fannie	13	F	" "	
1261	1272	347	Ross	Henry	35	M	" "	2160 Clifton roll
		Ind. Dist.						
1262	1273	350	"	Cardine	15	F	" "	Formerly Sanders wife of Joshua Ross.
		Ill. Dist.						
1263	1274	348	Riley	Charles	80	M	" "	1739 Clifton roll On Cher. roll as 50 in 1880
1264	1275	349	"	Esther	70	F	" "	1740 Clifton
1265	1276	351	"	William	13	M	" "	
1266	1277	356	Riley	Cicero	50	M	" "	
1267	1278	357	Ratcliffe	Allen	31	M	" "	
1268	1279	358	Ross	Hester	37	F	" "	

Authenticated Freedmen

Office No.	Woodhall No.	Number No.	Names		age	Sex	Residence	
1269	1280	Ill. Dist. 359	Rogers	Amanda	24	F	Illinois Dist.	1341 Clifton roll Wm Bryant, See Shelby's admitted list No. 619 for daughter Ellis, See No. 1450
1270	1281	Canadian Dist. 48	Snow	Daniel	50	M	" "	1606 Clifton roll
1271	1282	49	"	Ruth	43	F	" "	1607 "
1272	1283	52	"	Rose	13	F	" "	1610 "
1273	1284	54	"	Wilson	11	M	" "	1609 On Cher. roll "Wilee"
1274	1285	Ill. Dist. 579	Saddle	Blanket	50	M	" "	2425 Clifton roll
1275	1286	424	Smith	Maria	28	F	" "	1000 Clifton roll Formerly Thompson
1276	1287		"	Willie	7	M	" "	1001 Clifton roll
1277	1288	379	Shepherd	Wash	60	M	" "	1236 Clifton roll
1278	1289	380	"	Lydia	36	F	" "	1237
1279	1290	381	"	Maria	17	F	" "	1238
1280	1291	382	"	Joanna	12	F	" "	1006 Clifton roll
1281	1292	383	"	Mary	12	F	" "	"
1282	1293	384	"	Curtis	11	M	" "	1239 On Cher. roll "Carter"
1283	1294		"	Legal	8	M	" "	1240
1284	1295	364	Sanders	Susie	31	M	" "	Dead
1285	1296	365	"	Nora	28	F	" "	1197 Clifton roll
1286	1297	366	"	Sarah	11	F	" "	1198 " "
1287	1298		"	Clem	7	M	" "	1199 " "
1288	1299	153	Skales	Harriet	25	F	" "	988 Clifton roll Formerly Foreman
1289	1300	389	Smith	Jacob	30	M	" "	1972 Clifton

Authenticated Freedmen

Office No.	Dawes No.	Dawson No.		Names	age	Sex	Residence	
		Ill. Dist						
1290	1301	371	Smith	Robert	54	M	Illinois Dist	1082 Clifton roll
1291	1302	372	"	Malinda	54	F	" "	1083 On Cher. roll as "Jakey Smith"
1292	1303	374	"	Florence	20	F	" "	1084 " "
1293	1304	373	Smith	Robert Jr.	25	M	" "	
1294	1305	391	Starr	Oliver	45	M	" "	1151 Clifton roll
1295	1306	392	"	Eliza	41	F	" "	1152 "
1296	1307	393	"	Bertie or John	14	M/F	" "	1153 "
1297	1308		"	Samuel	9	M	" "	1154 "
1298	1309	370	Starr	Henry	34	M	" "	1052 Clifton roll
1299	1310	154	"	Martha	25	F	" "	1054 Formerly Freeman
1300	1311	360	Stidham	Sam	32	M	" "	895 Clifton roll
1301	1312	361	"	Dollie	28	F	" "	896 " "
1302	1313	362	"	Charles	11	M	" "	897 " "
1303	1314	363	"	Thomas	16	M	" "	895 On Cher. roll as William
1304	1315	Can. Dist 56	Shepherd	Coffee	56	M	" "	1216 Clifton roll
1305	1316	Ill. Dist 367	Smith	Delila	50	F	" "	2446 Clifton roll Died Oct. 1889
1306	1317	394	Smith	Thompson	90	M	" "	
1307	1318	395	"	Sophia	50	F	" "	
1308	1319	396	"	Sally	25	F	" "	1520 Clifton roll Same as 2732
1309	1320	397	Sanders	Rabbit	85	M	" "	1061 Clifton roll On Cher. roll as "45" in 1880
1310	1321	398	Stealer	James	35	M	" "	

Authenticated Freedmen

Off. No.	Roll No.	Number No.	Names		Age	Sex	Residence	
1311	1322	399 (Ill. Dist)	Smith	Polly	30	F	Illinois Dist	1370 Clifton roll
1312	1323	400	Smith	Sarah	35	F	" "	576 Clifton roll / Am. formerly Johnson
1313	1324	401	"	Julia	19	F	" "	577 Clifton roll / On Cher. roll as "Julu"
1314	1325	402	"	Ella	13	F	" "	Died before Mar. 3 '83 #14291 (91)
1315	1326	443	Thompson	Emma	29	F	" "	1551 Clifton roll
1316	1327		"	Sophia	7	F	" "	1553 " "
1317	1328	414	Thompson	Robt. Jr.	30	M	" "	1121 Clifton roll / 936 Clifton roll
1318	1329	418	"	Sylvia	31	F	" "	Formerly Thornton
1319	1330	419	"	John	16	M	" "	On Cher. roll as Thornton
1320	1331	420	"	Henrietta	15	F	" "	937 Clifton roll
1321	1332	421	"	Seymour	12	M	" "	938 " " "
1322	1333	422	"	Unice	10	F	" "	939 " " "
1323	1334	417	Thornton	Nancy	50	F	" "	935 Clifton roll
1324	1335	427	Thompson	Willie	23	M	" "	
1325	1336	433	Thompson	John	33	M	" "	
1326	1337	434	"	Sarah	45	F	" "	1208 Clifton roll
1327	1338	435	"	Levi	12	M	" "	1209 " "
1328	1339		"	Robert	8	M	" "	1212 " "
1329	1340	490	Tyner	Nancy	34	F	" "	Duplicate of #314 See 14291 (91) / See 315 Wallace
1330	1341	436	Tyner	Andrew	58	M	" "	
1331	1342	300	"	Emeline	30	F	" "	1783 Clifton roll / formerly Pinder

Authenticated Freedmen

Office No.	Muster No.	Employ No. 26 Dis.	Names		age	Sex	Residence	
1332	1343	444	Theodore	Lewis	55	M	Illinois Dist.	
1333	1344	406	Tally	Mollie	23	F	" "	
1334	1345	407	"	Penn	20	M	" "	
1335	1346	408	"	Sibod	18	M	" "	
1336	1347	409	"	Annie	13	F	" "	
1337	1348	416	Thompson	Moses	29	M	" "	1231 Clifton roll
1338	1349	423	Thompson	Alfred	36	M	" "	1600 " "
1339	1350	425	Thompson	Pompey	52	M	" "	1567 Clifton roll
1340	1351	429	"	Henry	19	M	" "	
1341	1352	430	"	Richard	16	M	" "	
1342	1353	431	"	Jeff	15	M	" "	1210 Clifton roll
1343	1354	428	Thompson	Edward	20	M	" "	
1344	1355	432	Tucker	Lewis	37	M	" "	1599 " "
1345	1356	Can Dist 41	Rider	Lovely	11	M & F	" "	1492 "
1346	1357	62	Thompson	Jeff	40	M	" "	Dead
1347	1358	63	"	Josephine	40	F	" "	
1348	1359	45	Silk	Anderson	17	M	" "	1438 Clifton roll
1349	1360	46	"	Squire	15	M	" "	
1350	1361	47	"	John	13	M	" "	1673 "
1351	1362	Conwes Dist 305	Tyner	Prince	28	M	" "	1337 Clifton roll
1352	1363	Ill Dist 291	"	Nancy	25	F	" "	10% " Clifton roll Formerly Nevins

Authenticated Freedmen

Office No	Wallace No	Number	Names		Age	Sex	Residence	
1353	1364	Ill. Dist. 538	Tyner	Sarah	18	F	Illinois Dist	Formerly Clifton Walker
1354	1365	491	Vann	Reed	23	M	" "	163✓ "
1355	1366	520	Vann	Sam	26	M	" "	1752 "
1356	1367	101	" or Vose	Lydia	27	F	" "	Formerly Cooper, Certif says Vose
1357	1368		"	David	8	M	" "	1753 Clifton roll
1358	1369	497	Vann	Butler	58	M	" "	1156 Clifton roll On Cherokee age 40 yrs in 1880
1359	1370	498	"	Sarah	45	F	" "	1157
1360	1371	501	"	Cynthia	21	F	" "	1826 "
1361	1372	502	"	James	18	M	" "	1679 "
1362	1373	503	"	Moses	17	M	" "	1073 "
1363	1374	504	"	Bud	16	M	" "	
1364	1375	505	"	Beckie	15	F	" "	1540 "
1365	1376	506	"	Alice	12	F	" "	1158
1366	1377	507	"	Eli	11	M	" "	1160 "
1367	1378		"	Linda	7	F	" "	1159
1368	1379	530	Vann	Solomon	40	M	" "	1377
1369	1380	445	"	Nelly	45	F	" "	Formerly Theodore
1370	1382	473	Vann	Polly	35	F	" "	1394 Clifton roll
1371	1383	478	"	Jacob	17	M	" "	1395 "
1372	1384	479	"	Bethuel	11	M	" "	1394a On Cher. roll "Belfnd"
1373	1385		"	Gnesie	8	M?	" "	1396b "
1374	1386		"	Peggy	7	F	" "	1397 "
1375	1387	492	Vann	Lincoln	20	M	" "	

Authenticated Freedmen

Office No.	Roll No.	Ill. Dist. No.	Names		Age	Sex	Residence		
1376	1388	466	Vann	Sank	40	M	Illinois Dist.	912	Clifton roll
1377	1389	467	"	Fannie	30	F	" "	913	"
1378	1390	468	"	Samuel	15	M	" "	914	"
1379	1391	469	"	Frank	11	M	" "	916	"
1380	1392		"	Sarah	9	F	" "	915	"
1381	1393	595	Vann	Lizzie	21	F	" "	Dead	
1382	1394	512	Vann	Cato	36	M	" "	1405 Clifton roll On Cher roll "Caty"	
1383	1395	513	"	Rachel	32	F	" "	1406 "	
1384	1396	514	"	Walter	14	M	" "	1407 "	
1385	1397	515	"	George	13	M		1408 "	
1386	1398	516	"	Mary	12	F	" "	1409 "	
1387	1399	517	"	Laura	10	F	" "	1410 "	
1388	1400		"	Roan	7	M	"		
1389	1401		Vann	Frank	35	M	" "	2636 "	
1390	1402		"	Beulah	8	F	" "	2637 "	
1391	1403		"	Lonnie	7	M	" "	2638 "	
1392	1404	522	Vann	Jack	36	M	" "	1794 "	
1393	1405	524	"	Lorda	100	F	" "	On Cher roll "Roda"	
1394	1406	527	"	Bass	40	M			
1395	1407	523	Vann	Martha	45	F	" "	1803 Clifton roll	
1396	1408		"	Russell	8	M	" "		
1397	1409	488	Vann	James	32	M	" "	1024 Clifton roll	
1398	1410	537	"	Nancy	24	F	" "	1025 Formerly Walker	

Authenticated Freedmen

Office No.	Enroll No.	Dawes No.		Names	age	Sex	Residence	
1399	1411	Ill. Dist. 489	Vann	David Jr.	31	M	Illinois Dist.	
1400	1412	490	Vann	George	27	M	" "	1138 Clifton Roll
1401	1413	249	"	Rosie	17	F	" "	1139 Formerly Mayfield
1402	1414	508	Vann	Rufus	22	M	" "	
1403	1415	509	Vann	Irving	37	M	" "	
1404	1416	511	"	Tom	22	M	" "	
1405	1417	525	Vann	Daniel	23	M	" "	1327 Clifton Roll
1406		Tah. Dist. 353	"	Ida	24	F	" "	1328 Formerly "Smith"
1407	1418	Ill. Dist. 528	Vann	Joseph E.	39	M	" "	
1408	1419	529	Vann	John	19	M	" "	1095 Clifton Roll
1409	1420	532	Vann	Cynthia	26	F	" "	1827 "
1410	1421	454	Vann	Mannel	21	M	" "	981 Clifton Roll
1411	1422	456	"	Major	17	M	" "	289 "
1412	1423	457	Vann	Crow	49	M	" "	1418 "
1413	1424	461	"	Simon	15	M	" "	"
1414	1425	462	"	Jennie	12	F	" "	
1415	1426	460	Vann	Lydia	17	F	" "	
1416	1427	493 465	Vann	Hannah alias Julia	22	F	See 29668 (493) "	900 Clifton Roll

Paid 60 No 1934

Same as 1934 wade intended to have left Wallace, changed her name on their list from Julia to Hannah, also the name be dropped & let Julia stick to Clifton

Authenticated Freedmen

Office No.	Williams No.	Census No.	Names		Age	Sex	Residence	
1417	1428	Ill. Dist. 470	Vann	Caleb	80	M	Illinois Dist.	
1418	1429	472	"	Sally	50	F	" "	
1419	1430	477	"	Emma	25	F	" "	
1420	1431	476	"	Fannie	22	F	" "	
1421	1432	474	"	Belle	36	F	" "	1089 Clifton roll
1422	1433	480	"	Cora	14	F	" "	1090 "
1423	1434	481	"	Adalaide	13	F	" "	1091 "
1424	1435	482	"	David	12	M	" "	1092 "
1425	1436	521	Vann	Richard	10	M	" "	1716 "
1426	1437		Wright	Henry	8	M	" "	
1427	1438	Can. Dist. 64	Vann	John Budie	29	M	" "	Dup. of 812
1428	1439		"	Lulu	7	F	" "	
1429	1440	Ill. Dist. 547	Webber	Dugald	64	M	" "	891 Clifton roll
1430	1441	548	"	Katie	34	F	" "	892 " "
1431	1442	549	"	Amanda	14	F	" "	893 " "
1432	1443		Watie	Joseph	43	M	" "	2787 Dup. See 1972
1433	1444	562	"	Martha	34	F	" "	1534 Clifton roll
1434	1445	564	"	David	16	M	" "	1535 "
1435	1446	565	"	Frances	14	F	" "	
1436	1447	566	Walker	Fannie	38	F	" "	1630 "
1437	1448	567	"	Leo	14	M	" "	
1438	1449	568	"	William	16	M	" "	
1439	1450	570	Williams	Ned	29	M	" "	

Authenticated Freedmen

Office No	Wallace No	Cherokee No	Names		age	Sex	Residence	
1440	1451	Ill.Dist. 543	Watie	Thomas	40	M	Illinois Dist.	1163 Clifton road
1441	1452	544	"	Winta	42	F	" "	1164 " "
1442	1453	545	"	Keller	12	M	" "	On Cher. roll as "Cda"
1443	1454	646	"	Walter	10	M	" "	1165 " "
1444	1455		"	Everett	8	M	" "	1166 "
1445	1456	535	Walker	Thos. H	35	M	" "	870 Clifton road
1446	1457	536	"	Moses	27	M	" "	869 Clifton road
1447	1458	59	"	Dinah	34	F	" "	871 Formerly Crapo
1448	1459	875	Sanders	Anderson	16	M	" "	872 "
1449	1460	376(a)	"	Lucy	14	F	" "	873
1450	1461	376(b)	"	Hannah	11	F	" "	874 "
1451	1462		Vann	Ellis	7	M	"	875
1452	1463	599	Woodard	James	35	M	"	884 Clifton wife of same Rogers
1453	1464	602	"	Susan	13	F	"	887 Clifton
1454	1465	284	McCoy	Waddie	14	M	" "	On Cher roll as "Mollie"
1455	1466	604	Woodard	Charles	26	M	" "	803 Clifton road
								1100 Clifton road
1456	1467	234	Williams	Matilda	44	F	" "	Formerly Lipe
1457	1468	533	Vann	Margaret	17	F	" "	
1458	1469	560	Williams	Jennie	14	F	" "	1094 Clifton road
1459	1470	561	"	Henry	11	M	" "	1097 "
1460	1471	571	"	Lewis	10	M	" "	1101 "
1461	1472	233	Lipe	Margaret	70	F	" "	

Authenticated Freedmen

Office No	Woollen No	Colored No	Names		age	Sex	Residence	
1462	1473	Ill Dist 540	Walker	Betsey	30	F	Illinois Dist	1028 Clifton rail
1463	1474	541	"	Violet	14	F	" "	1029 "
1464	1475	542	"	Elizabeth	10	F	" "	1030 "
1465	1476		"	Newton	7	M	" "	1031 "
1466	1477½	278	Welch	Sadie	15	F	" "	1367 Formerly "McKee
1467	1477	Tahl Dist 2	Alberty	David	40	M	Tahlequah Dist	1103 Clifton rail
1468	1478	5	Alberty	Delila	14	F	" "	1106 Clifton rail 1500 "
1469	1479	354	Smith	Annie	65	F	" "	See 2805
470	1480	3	Alberty	Bony	26	M	" "	1104 Clifton rail
471	1481	6	"	Lelah	11	F	" "	1107 "
472	1482	222	Austin	Emeline	27	F	" "	Formerly McCracken
473	1483		"	Lewis	10	M	" "	1017 Clifton rail
474	1484		"	Robt	9	M	" "	1018 "
475	1485		"	Hannibal	7	M	" "	
476	1486	Ill Dist 16	Brewer	Andy	44	M	" "	1039 Clifton rail 1046
477	1487	Tahl Dist 16(b)	"	Charlotte	25	F	" "	Formerly "Harlin
478	1488	7	Brewer +	Rabb	40	M	" "	750 Clifton rail on Cher. roll "Bob
479	1489	8	"	Elsie	60	F	" "	
80	1490	9	— Betsey —		50	F	" "	
81	1492	Ill Dist 130	Burges	Jennie	34	F	" "	1031 Clifton rail Formerly Davis
82	1494	Tahl Dist 11	"	John	36	M	" "	1030 Clifton rail

Authenticated Freedmen

Office No.	Dawes No.	Census No.		Names	Age	Sex	Residence	
		Teh.Dist.						
1483	1495	12	Buffington	Ambrose	30	M	Tahlequah Dist.	On Cher. roll "Ambus"
1484	1496	333	"	Nancy	24	F	" "	Formerly Rogers.
1485	1497	13	Bean	Henry	38	M	" "	2090 Clifton roll
1486	1498	14	"	Frances	37	F	" "	2091
1487	1499	429	Whitmire	Charles	20	M	" "	
1488	1500	15	Bean	Sarah	13	F	" "	2092 "
1489	1501	16	"	Willie	10	M	" "	2093 "
1490	1502	18	Buffington	Darkey	63	F	" "	1233 Clifton roll
1491	1503	19	"	Ambrose	14	M	" "	On Cher. roll "Ambus"
1492	1504	21	Buffington	Joseph	45	M	" "	
1493	1505	27	Buffington	Margaret	40	F	" "	1300 Clifton roll
1494	1506	137	Gentry	George	14	M	" "	2247 " "
1495	1507		Brown	Joseph	45	M	" "	1374 Clifton roll
1496	1508	22	"	Josephine	38	F	" "	1374 Clifton roll
1497	1509	23	"	Sophia	13	F	" "	1372 "
1498	1510	24	"	Hubbard	10	M	" "	1373 "
1499	1511		"	Charles	7	M	" "	1375 "
1500	1512	28	Beck	James	75	M	" "	959 Clifton roll
1501	1513	29	"	Jennie	52	F	" "	
1562	1514	30	"	Sylvia	25	F	" "	960 "
1503	1515	31	"	Jim	21	M	" "	961 On Cher. roll "Jennie"
1564	1516	33	"	Carrie	15	F	" "	962 "

Authenticated Freedmen

Officer No.	Roll No.	Chraky No.	Names		age	sex	Residence	
		Tah. Dist.						
1505	1517	34	Brady	Barney	60	M	Tahlequah Dist.	1200 Clifton roll
1506	1518	35	"	Maria	60	F	" "	" "
1507	1519	36	Bean	Dock	15	M	" "	1262 "
1508	1520	37	Bean	Louisa	31	F	" "	2457 Clifton
1509	1521	38	"	Pate	15	M	" "	2458 "
1510	1522	39	"	White	10	F	" "	2459 " "
1511	1523		"	Jackson	7	M	" "	
1512	1524	4	Alberty	Sallie	29	F	" "	1105 Clifton roll
1513	1525	40	Bean	Mary	22	F	" "	
1514	1526	41	"	Christy	18	F	" "	
1515	1527	42	"	Sarah	16	F	" "	1299 "
1516	1528	45	Brewer	Jackson	14	M	" "	1676 "
1517	1529	43	Brewer	Fannie	21	F	" "	
1518	1530	47	Bean	Sarah	34	F	" "	
1519	1531	48	"	Annie	13	F	" "	1191 Clifton roll
1520	1532		"	Mary	7	F	" "	1264 "
1521	1533	100	Bird	Susan	22	F	" "	2001 Formerly Evans
1522	1534		"	Amanda	7	F	" "	2003 "
1523	1535		"	Henrietta	8	F	" "	2002 "
1524	1536	104	Evans	Martha	16	F	" "	
1525	1537	Cooweescoowee Dist. 325	Bryant	Sophia	32	F	" "	310 Clifton roll Formerly Evans
1526	1538	Tah. Dist. 62	Carter	Maud	19	F	" "	

Authenticated Freedmen

Office No.	Roll No.	Chero. No.	Names		Age	Sex	Residence		
		Tah Dist.							
1527	1539	51	Cornice	Fannie	65	F	Tahlequah Dist.		
1528	1540	381	Saunders	George	16	M	"	"	2442 Clifton coll.
1529	1541	52	Campbell	Nelson	33	M	"	"	2081 Clifton roll
1530	1542	114	"	Martha	24	F	"	"	Formerly Fields
1531	1543		"	Jack	9	M	"	"	2082 "
1532	1544		"	Katie	7	F	"	"	2083 "
1533	1545	53	Campbell	Sophia	69	F	"	Cudeo 3242	2192 "
1534	1546	58	Carter	Arch	46	M	"	"	1469 Clifton roll
1535	1547	59	"	Sarah	43	F	"	"	1470 "
1536	1548	61	"	Moses	20	M	"	"	1207 Clifton roll
1537	1549	63	"	Joe	18	M	"	"	1472 "
1538	1550	64	"	Mank	16	M	"	"	On Cher. roll "Amanda"
1539	1551	65	"	Cora	13	F	"	"	1473 "
1540	1552	66	"	William	11	M	"	"	1474 "
1541	1553	67	"	Minnie	10	F	"	"	1475 "
1542	1554		"	Johnson	8	M	"	"	1476 "
1543	1555	68	Carter	Nelson	34	M	"	"	2419 Clifton roll
1544	1556	69	"	Mary	32	F	"	"	2424 "
1545	1557	70	"	Belle	18	F	"	"	2420 "
1546	1558	71	"	Jennie	15	F	"	"	
1547	1559	72	"	Senah	11	F	"	"	2422 Clifton roll
1548	1560	73	"	George	10	M	"	"	2423 "
1549	1561		"	Henry	6	M	"	"	2421 "

Authenticated Freedmen

Official No.	Gallows No.	Election No.	Names		Age	Sex	Residence		
		Tah. Dist.							
1550	1562	74	Carter	Lewis	40	M	Tahlequah Dist.	2056	Clifton roll
1551	1563	75	"	Maria	45	F	"	"	2057	"
1552	1564	76	"	Andy	20	M	"	"	2058	
1553	1565	77	"	Rachel	18	F	"	"	For children see 2003-4 Clifton roll
1554	1566	78	"	Dick	13	M	"	"	2061	"
1555	1567	79	"	Calvin	11	M	"	"	2062	"
1556	1568		"	David	8	M	"	"	2059	"
1557	1569	80	— Cynthia —		45	F	"	"		
1558	1570	83	Collins	Chaney n Chaney	29	F	"	"	2224 clifton roll
1559	1571		"	Ross	9	M	"	"	
1560	1572		"	Abraham	7	M	"	"	
1561	1573	81	Clifton	Anthony	50	M	"	"	2223 clifton roll
1562	1574	84	Cates	Narcissa	35	F	"	"	1831 Clifton roll
1563	1575	85	"	Florence	15	F	"	"	1832	"
1564	1576	86	"	Sally	13	F	"	"	1833	"
1565	1577	87	"	Ada	11	F	"	"	1834	"
1566	1578	88	"	Thomas	10	M	"	"	1835	"
1567	1579		"	Lucy	7	F	"	"	1836	"
1568	1580		Thompson	Johnson	7	M	"	"	Born after Mar 3 '63 14291(91) Born in fall 1863 14705(91) 7031(91)
1569	1581	90	Campbell	Alick	47	M	"	"	
1570	1562	431	Clark	Charles	36	M	"	"	

Authenticated Freedmen

Office No	Wallace 350	Wardour 450 Col. Dist	Names		age	Sex	Residence	
1571	1583	93	Dennis	Patsey	38	F	Tahlequah Dist	1527 Clifton roll
1572	1584	94	"	Florence	18	F	" "	1528 "
1573	1585	95	"	Junius	17	M	" "	1529 "
1574	1586		"	Emma	8	F	" "	
1575	1587		Brown	Fannie	20	F	" "	
1576	1588	97	Davis	Rose	12	F	" "	3648 "
1577	1589	110	Eagle	Eliza	32	F	" "	2042 "
1578	1590	311	Ross	Moses	14	M	" "	
1579	1591	144	Hailstock	Charles	11	M	" "	2043 "
1580	1592		Luther	Jack	7	M	" "	2044 "
1581	1593	108	Eagle	Julia	38	F	" "	
1582	1594	109	Eagle	Pauline	60	F	" "	2041 "
1583	1595	99	Evans	Mary	45	F	" "	2071 Clifton roll
1584	1596	161	"	Malinda	21	F	" "	2079 Clifton roll
1585	1597	102	"	William	19	M	" "	2072 Clifton
1586	1598	103	"	Phillis	15	F	" "	2073 "
1587	1599	165	"	Jane	13	F	" "	2074 "
1588	1600	44	Ford	Carrie	17	F	" "	1695 Clifton roll formerly Brewer
1589	1601	116	Fields	Michael	21	M	" "	1354 clifton roll
1590	1602	273	"	Carrie	17	F	" "	2676 formerly Pack
1591	1603	432	Fields	Annie	37	F	" "	2113 Clifton roll

Authenticated Freedmen

Office No	Dawson No	Tahlequah Dist	Names		age	Sex	Residence		
1592	1604	115	Fields	Jerry	46	M	Tahlequah Dist	1353	Clifton roll
1593	1605	112	Fields	Simon	43	M	" "	1984	"
1594	1606	113	"	Katie	42	F	" "	1983	" "
1595	1607	118	"	John	21	M	" "	1990	"
1596	1608	121	"	Phobe	15	F	" "		
1597	1609	122	"	Annie	12	F	" "	1986	"
1598	1610		"	Simon Jr	10	M	" "	1984	"
1599	1611	123	Grimmett	Clark	45	M	" "	963	Clifton red
1600	1612	124	"	Peggy	45	F	" "	964	"
1601	1613	125	"	Lila	21	F	" "	965	"
1602	1614	126	"	Henderson	13	M	" "	966	"
1603	1615	127	"	John	11	M	" "	967	"
1604	1616		"	Sandy	8	M	" "	968	"
1605	1617	128	Goff	Matilda	54	F	" "	1981	"
1606	1618	131	Green	Easter	50	F	" "		
1607	1619	132	"	Alex	13	M	" "		
1608	1620	134	Gentry	Maria	38	F	" "	2244	Clifton roll
1609	1621	138	"	Florence	12	F	" "	2248	" "
1610	1622	139	"	Lizzie	10	F	" "	2249	" "
1611	1623		"	Carrie	7	F	" "		
1612	1624	136	Gentry	Amanda	18	F	" "	2246	Clifton roll
1613	1625	141	Griffin	Nathan	35	M	" "	2240	Clifton roll
1614	1626	142	"	Amanda	14	F	" "	2241	" "

Authenticated Freedmen

Office No	Enrollment No	Census No	Names		age	Sex	Residence		
1615	1627	143 Reb Dist	Grimmett	Benj	32	M	Tahlequah Dist	2130 Clifton	
1616	1628	433	Grimmett	Rachel	27	F	"	"	1970 Clifton
1617	1629	389	Hawkins	Annie	21	F	"	"	1697 Clifton roll Formerly Taylor
1618	1630	145	Hildebrand	Nancy	34	F	"	"	
1619	1631	146	Henson	Harry	40	M	"	"	
1620	1632	147	Humphries	Richard	64	M	"	"	
1621	1633	397	"	Emily	57	F	"	"	3960 Clifton roll Formerly Vann
1622	1634	149	"	Julia	23	F	"	"	1313 Clifton roll
1623	1635		"	Martha	10	F	"	"	2129 "
1624	1636	150	Humphries	Peter	42	M	"	"	Died March 21, 1890
1625	1637		"	Alice	33	F	"	"	
1626	1638		"	Joseph	7	M	"	"	
1627	1639	159	Hicks	Robert	27	M	"	"	2228 Clifton roll
1628	1640	395	"	Martha	35	F	"	"	2229 Clifton roll Formerly Vann
1629	1641	160	Hicks	Jack	26	M	"	"	
1630	1642	161a	Hartin	Bass	47	M	"	"	1888 Clifton roll
1631	1643	163	"	Solomon	20	M	"	"	1891 Clifton roll
1632	1644	164	"	Cornelius	18	M	"	"	On other roll "Neeley"
1633	1645	165	"	Clem	14	M	"	"	1893 "

Authenticated Freedmen

			Names		Age	Sex	Residence	
1634	1646	166	Harlin	Thomas	45	M	Tahlaquah Dist	1896 Clifton roll
1635	1647	171	"	Joseph	17	M	" "	1898 "
1636	1648	172	"	Harry	15	M	" "	1899 "
1637	1649	173	"	Ben	12	M	" "	1900 "
1638	1650	174	"	Howard	10	M	" "	1901 "
1639	1651	168	Harlin	John	22	M	" "	1897 "
1640	1652	169	Harlin	Darkey	20	F	" "	
1641	1653	400	Hicks	Martha	46	F	" "	1178 Clifton roll / Formerly Vann
1642	1654	402	Vann	Looney	18	M	" "	
1643	1655	403	"	Annie	15	F	" "	1172 "
1644	1656	404	"	James	14	M	" "	1175 "
1645	1657	405	"	Peggy	12	F	" "	1173 "
1646	1658	406	"	John	10	M	" "	1176 "
1647	1659		"	Ella	9	F	" "	1177 "
1648	1660	178	Irons	Ned	33	M	" "	1939
1649	1661	436	"	Julia	31	F	" "	Formerly Pettit
1650	1662		"	Jerry J.	7	M	" "	1941
1651	1663	179	Irons	Katie	34	F	" "	
1652	1664	180	Irons	John	33	M	" "	2047 "
1653	1665	181	"	Martha	29	F	" "	2048 "
1654	1666	182	"	Eliza	10	F	" "	2049 "
1655	1667	434	Irons	Andy	26	M	" "	

Authenticated Freedmen

Office No	Wallace No	Shuler No		Names	age	Sex	Residence	
1656	1668	Saline Dist. 41	Jones	Alice	24	F	Tahlequah Dist	512 Clifton Roll Formerly Johnson
1657	1669	40	Johnson	Amanda	46	F	" "	517 Clifton Roll
1658	1670	37	Johnson	Even	36	M	" "	1992 "
1659	1671	Tah Dist 120	"	Lucy	17	F	" "	Formerly Fields
1660	1672	Saline Dist 38	Johnson	Eliza	76	F	" "	Mother of 1662
1661	1673	39	"	Even	14	M	" "	1993 Clifton roll
1662	1674	46	Johnson	Murrell	38	M	" "	1850 Clifton roll
1663	1675	47	"	Martha	34	F	" "	1847 Clifton roll
1664	1676	48	"	Maud	11	F	" "	1848 "
1665	1677		"	George M.	8	M	" "	1849 "
1666	1678	42	Johnson	Frog	45	M	" "	2020 On Cher. roll "Tong"
1667	1679	44	"	John	12	M	" "	569 Clifton Roll On Cher. roll "Johnson"
1668	1680	45	"	Andy	10	M	" "	568 Clifton roll
1669	1681	Tah Dist 184	Johnson	Sandy	43	M	" "	1181 Clifton roll
1670	1682	185	"	Malinda	33	F	" "	1182 " "
1671	1683	199	Johnson	Grace	35	F	" "	
1672	1684	Flint Dist 2	Johnson	Wiley	27	F	" "	2235 Clifton roll
1673	1685	3	"	Andrew	13	M	" "	2237 " "
1674	1686	4	"	Walter	11	M	" "	2236 " "
1675	1687		"	Lincoln	8	M	" "	2238 " "
1676	1688	1	Johnson	Adelaide	64	F		

Authenticated Freedmen

Office No.	Authen. No.	Chacters No.	Names		Age	Sex	Residence	
		Tah. Dist.						
1677	1689	194	Johnson	Si	33	M	Tahlequah Dist	1565 Clifton roll
1678	1690	195	"	Cinda	30	F	" "	1566 " "
1679	1691	196	"	Frank	14	M	" "	1567 " "
1680	1692		"	Tobey	7	M	" "	1568 "
1681	1693	188	Johnson	Moses	35	M	" "	900 Clifton roll
1682	1694	189	"	Mary	30	F	" "	901 "
1683	1695	190	"	Ben	16	M	" "	902 "
1684	1696	191	"	Martha	15	F	" "	903 "
1685	1697	192	"	Jennie	13	F	" "	904 "
1686	1698		"	July	7	F	" "	905 "
1687	1699	98	Johnson	Nathan	27	M	" "	2208 "
1688	1700	60	"	Martha	24	F	" "	2209 formerly Carter
1689	1701	414	Johnson	Hannah	36	F	" "	2189 formerly Webber
1690	1702	321	Johnson	Harriet	26	F	" "	2024 Clifton formerly Ross
1691	1703	157	Holt	George	12	M	" "	2025 "
1692	1704	158	"	Edmond	11	M	" "	2027 "
1693	1705		Johnson	Lawrence	7	M	" "	2028 "
		Tequah Dist.						
1694	1706	57	Johnson	Thomas	16	M	" "	
		Tah. Dist.						
1695	1707	200	Keyes	Jonas James	38	M	" "	
1696	1708	201	Keys	George	29	M	" "	1640 Clifton roll

Authenticated Freedmen

Office No.	Wallace No.	Kern No.	Names		Age	Sex	Residence		
1697	1709	Tah. Dist. 204	Lipe	Jack	80	M	Tahlequah Dist	2197	Clifton roll
1698	1710	205	"	Mary	60	F	" "	2198	" "
1699	1711	206	"	William	21	M	" "		
1700	1712	213	Lowery	Jennetta	17	F	" "	1081	Clifton roll
1701	1713	Saline Dist. 103	Luther	Lizzie	31	F	" "	For Clifton roll Formerly Vann	
1702	1714		"	Annie	7	F	" "	1958	Clifton roll
1703	1715	Tah Dist 203	Lowrey	Nelson	31	M	" "	2086	"
1704	1716		"	Ella	6	F	" "	2087	"
1705	1717	207	Lasley	Columbus	38	M	" "	2101	"
1706	1718	208	"	Peggy	34	F	" "	2102	"
1707	1719	209	"	Willie	14	M	" "	2103	"
1708	1720	210	"	Pearlie	11	F	" "	2104	"
1709	1721		"	Charles	9	M	" "	2105	"
1710	1722	214	Lasley	Andy	30	M	" "	921 Clifton roll	
1711	1723	221	"	Lucy	30	F	" "	Formerly Hildebrand	
1712	1724	215	"	Hannah	80	F	" "		
1713	1725	216	Mosely	Rhoda	27	F	" "	2038 Clifton roll	
1714	1726	217	McCoy	Dollie	80	F	" "	924 to Lipe body Admr	
1715	1727	218	Marshall	Jeff	36	M	" "		
1716	1728	223	McCracken	Nancy	25	F	" "	1015 Clifton roll	

Authenticated Freedmen

Office No.	Wallace No.	Clerks No. (Sch. Dist.)	Names		age	Sex	Residence	
1717	1729	224	McCracken	Andy	24	M	Tahlequah Dist	2182 Clifton roll
1718	1730	233	Madden	Mary	26	F	" "	1953 Clifton roll
1719	1731	234	"	Annie	11	F	" "	1954 " "
1720	1732	235	Macon	Auth.	35	11	" "	
1721	1733	236	"	John	11	M	" "	
1722	1734	238	McCoy	Jinnie	60	F	" "	
1723	1735	240	Mayes	Berry	61	M	" "	1221 Clifton roll.
1724	1736	177	Manach	Frances	29	F	" "	1422 Clifton roll Formerly Hildebrand
1725	1737	418	Wilson	Manuel	14	M	" "	1454 Clifton roll
1726	1738	419	"	Amanda	11	F	" "	1455 "
1727	1739	420	"	Angeline	10	F	" "	1456 "
~~1728~~	~~1740~~		~~Manach~~	~~Wallace~~	7	M	" "	Creek — did not desire to draw (90) 14291.
1729	1741		Thompson	Henry	8	M	" "	1425 Clifton roll M.921 Son of Minnie Thompson No. 252
1730	1742	162	McConnell	Sally	22	F	" "	888 Clifton roll Formerly Harlin
1731	1743		Meadows	Mary	26	F	" "	nee Pack now Sumter 2241 Clifton roll
1732	1744		"	Nannie	10	F	" "	2242 Clifton roll
1733	1745	237	Meigs	Sam	38	M	" "	2044b Clifton roll 2945b
1734	1746	421	"	Ida or Ada	30	F	" "	Formerly Whitmire
1735	1747	422	Whitmire	Alice	16	F	" "	2046b "
1736	1748		Meigs	Robt.	8	M	" "	2047b "
1737	1749	256	McIntosh	Josephine	14	F	" "	956 Clifton roll Formerly Nevens

Authenticated Freedmen

Office No	Roll No	Number on	Names		age	Sex	Residence	
		Tah Dist						
1738	1750	220	McCracken	George	45	M	Tahlequah Dist	N 80 Clifton roll
1739	1751	221	"	Rose	46	F	" "	2181
1740	1752	225	"	Pompey	21	M	" "	2182 "
1741	1753	226	"	Sylvia	20	F	" "	2184 "
1742	1754	228	"	Sarah	15	F	" "	2185 "
1743	1755	229	"	Daniel	10	M	" "	2186 "
1744	1756		"	Jesse	7	M	" "	2187 "
1745	1757	242	Nave	Jane	44	F	" "	
1746	1758	243	"	Thomas	12	M	" "	
1747	1759	248	Nave	John	24	M	" "	Insane
1748	1760	247	Nave	Benjamin	25	M	" "	68 Clifton roll
1749	1761	315	"	Sarah	19	F	" "	2042 Formerly Ross
1750	1762	253	Kivens	Alex	45	M	" "	969 Clifton roll
1751	1763	254	"	Mary	39	F	" "	970 "
1752	1764	257	"	Richard	15	M	" "	972 "
1753	1765	258	"	Callis	13	M	" "	973 "
1754	1766	259	"	Harrison	11	M	" "	974 "
1755	1767		"	Sam	8	M	" "	975 "
1756	1768		"	Charles	7	M	" "	976 "
1757	1769	288 (Tah Dist)	Nave	Henry	24	M	" "	
1758	1770	271 (Tah Dist)	Pack	Martha	57	F	" "	
1759	1771	273	"	Henry	19	M	" "	1995 "
1760	1772	135	Parris	Frances	17	F		no 45 Clifton roll Formerly Gentry

Authenticated Freedmen

Office No.	Wallace Roll	Cherokee Roll Jel. Dist.	Names		age	Sex	Residence		
1761	1773	261	Parris	James	40	M	Tahlequah Dist.	1881	Clifton roll
1762	1774	262	"	Serena	40	F	"	"	1882	"
1763	1775	263	"	Anthony	18	M	"	"	1883	"
1764	1776	264	"	Jane	15	F	"	"	1868	Clifton roll
1765	1777	265	"	Henry	14	M	"	"	1885	"
1766	1778	266	"	Willi.	10	M	"	"	1886	"
1767	1779		"	Thomas	8	M	"	"	1887	
1768	1780	274	Jack	Frank	28	M		"	1924	"
1769	1781	275	"	Julia	25	F		"	1925	
1770	1782	276	"	Wm H	10	M		"	1926	"
1771	1783		"	Lizzie	8	F		"	1927	"
1772	1784		Parris	Caleb	40	M	"	"	2775	"
1773	1785		"	Lucy	60	F	"	"		
1774	1786	267	Pettit	George	35	M	"	"	1306	Clifton roll
1775	1787	268	"	Phillis	26	F	"	"	1307	"
1776	1788	269	"	Samuel	13	M	"	"	1308	"
1777	1789		"	Fish	8	F	"	"	13.09	"
1778	1790	392	Perryman	Patsey	28	F	"	"	4645 Formerly Taylor	
1779	1791	388	Taylor	Judy	65	F	"	"	4696	Clifton roll
1780	1792	318	Ross	Isaac	57	M	"	"		
1781	1793	319	"	Roanna	57	F	"	"		"
1782	1794	322	"	Stephen	20	M	"	"	2239	Clifton roll
1783	1795	332	Rogers	Betsey	25	F	"	"	3183	"

Authenticated Freedmen

3ffice no	Dawes no	Col. Dist no	Names		age	Sex	Residence		
1784	1796	334	Ratcliffe	Eliza	70	F	Tahlequah Dist.	See in Clifton roll No 2364 and letter 15 Mess Whitmire chro. 33, 91 226/154 also to Bennett " " " 226/153
1785	1797	335	Riley	Carla	90	F	"	"	
1786	1798	279	Ross	Lawrence	32	M	"	"	2037b Clifton
1787	1799	280	"	Moses	31	M	"	"	2054 b "
1788	1800	281	"	Sam	31	M	"	"	On Cher. roll "Ham"
1789	1801	282	Ross	Jack	50	M	"	"	2196 Clifton roll
1790	1802	284	Ross	Samuel	58	M	"	"	Pd to Stick Ross adm
1791	1803	285	"	Mary	35	F	"	"	Dead
1792	1804	289	Ross	Moses	55	M	"	"	219 3 Clifton roll
1793	1805	290	"	Becky	44	F	"	"	2194 "
1794	1806	293	"	Jack	22	M	"	"	2195 "
1795	1807	297	Ross	Edmond	70	M	"	"	
1796	1808	89	Cooper	Lim	14	M	"	"	
1797	1809	303	Ross	Benjamin	66	M	"	"	
1798	1810	313	"	Rose	67	F	"	"	
1799	1811	305	"	Mary	17	F	"	"	2163 Clifton roll
1800	1812	307	"	Aaron	15	M	"	"	2164 "
1801	1813	312	Ross	Thomas	39	M	"	"	
1802	1814	316	Ross	Dinah	37	F	"	"	2136 Clifton
1803	1815	317	"	Maggie	17	F	"	"	2040b Clifton roll

Authenticated Freedmen

Office No.	Collace No.	Cherokee No.	Names		age	sex	Residence		
		Tah. Dist.							
1804	1816		Rogers	Cephas	40	M	Tahlequah Dist.		
1805	1817		Ross	Joseph	34	M	"	"	2558 Clifton roll
1806	1818		"	Patsey	15	F	"	"	2560 "
1807	1819		"	Robert	12	M	"	"	2561 "
1808	1820		"	Lizzie	10	F	"	"	2562 "
1809	1821		"	Jane	7	F	"	"	2563 "
1810	1822	323	Ross	Sarah	40	F	"	"	1976 Clifton
1811	1823	324	"	Thomas	20	M	"	"	1923 Clifton roll
1812	1824	50	Cooper	William	15	M	"	"	1977 "
1813	1825	155	Humphries	Rich'd Jr	14	M	"	"	
1814	1826	156	"	Mollie	11	F	"	"	1978 "
1815	1827	437	Ross	John	24	M	"	"	2243 Clifton roll.
1816	1828	119	"	Peggie	20	F	"	"	Formerly Fields
1817	1829	277	Ross	Joseph	34	M	"	"	
1818	1830	176	"	Rhoda	26	F	"	"	Formerly Hicks
1819	1831	398	Vann	Alexander	20	M	"	"	2222 Clifton roll
1820	1832		Ross	Jennie A.	10	F	"	"	
1821	1833	308	Ross	Joseph	32	M	"	"	1930 Clifton roll
1822	1834	309	"	Laura	33	F	"	"	1931 "
1823	1835	310	"	Jodie	10	M	"	"	1932 "
1824	1836		"	Alex	9	M	"	"	1933 "
1825	1837		"	Jimmie	7	M	"	"	1934 "
1826	1838	320	Ross	Moses	29	M	"	"	

Unauthenticated Freedmen

Office No.	Comm'n Office No.	Chamber No. / Sub Dist.	Names		age	sex	Residence	
1827	1839	295	Ross	William	33	M	Tahlequah Dist.	3670 Clifton roll
1828	1840	296	"	Mary	23	F	" "	2126 Clifton roll
1829	1841		Grimmutt	Mary	7	F	" "	2127 "
1830	1842	299	Ross	Ned	39	M	" "	1963 Clifton
1831	1843	300	"	Ann	35	F	" "	1964 "
1832	1844	301	"	Lucy	12	F	" "	1965 Clifton roll
1833	1845	302	"	Lewis	11	M	" "	1968
1834	1846		"	Isaac	8	M	" "	
1835	1847		"	Hannie	7	F	" "	
1836	1848	278	Ross	Moses	31	M	" "	2172 "
1837	1849	117	"	Mary	23	F	" "	2173 Formerly "Fields
1838	1850	291	Ross	Edmond	22	M	" "	1905 Clifton roll
1839	1851	55	Ross	Lottie	45	F	" "	2150 Formerly "Campbell
1840	1852	56	Campbell	Eliza J.	16	F	" "	2148 Clifton
1841	1853	326	Rogers	Joseph	41	M	" "	1819 Clifton
1842	1854	328	"	Malinda	18	F	" "	1820 On Cher. roll "Linda"
1843	1855	329	"	Josie	16	F	" "	1822 "
1844	1856	330	"	Laura	11	F	" "	1821 On Cher. roll "Louisa"
1845	1857	260	Parris	Sarah	75	F	" "	
1846	1858		Rogers	Gabe	7	M	" "	1823 Clifton roll

Authenticated Freedmen

Office No	Tallequah No	Cherokee No	Names		age	Sex	Residence		
		Salina Dist.							
1847	1859	87	Ross	Joseph (Stick)	39	M	Tahlequah Dist.	1945	Clifton roll
1848	1860	88	"	Nancy	36	F	" "	1946	"
1849	1861	89	"	Austin	20	M	" "	1947	"
1850	1862		"	Malcolm	9	M	" "	1948	"
1851	1863		"	Julia	7	F	" "	1950	"
		Ill. Dist.							
1852	1864	346	Roach	Roller	63	?	" "	1895 Clifton	
1853	1865		Smith	Charley	34	M	" "		"
		Sal. Dist.							
1854	1866	325	"	Betsey	25	F	" "	Formerly Rogers	
1855	1867		McIntosh	Rink	7	M	" "	2701 Clifton roll	
1856	1868	343	Starr	Amanda	27	F	" "	1998 Clifton roll	
1857	1869	352	Smith	Ibby	35	F	" "	1498 Clifton roll	
1858	1870	351	"	Wash	12	M	" "	1499 "	
1859	1871		"	Pearlie	10	F	" "	1506 "	
1860	1872	283	Sells	Anna	35	F	" "	20913 Formerly Ross	
1861	1873	359	Shepherd	Joseph alt Joshua	55	M	" "	2067 Clifton roll	
1862	1874	360	"	Betsey	46	F	" "		
1863	1875	364	"	Ellen	16	F	" "	1910 Clifton	
1864	1876	365	"	Andrew	14	M	" "	2031b "	
1865	1877	366	"	Simon	12	M	" "	2032b "	
1866	1878	367	"	Nancy	10	F	" "	2033b "	
1867	1879		"	Minta	8	F	" "	2034b "	

Authenticated Freedmen

			Names		age	Sex	Residence		
1868	1880	Tah. Dist.	Shepherd	Morris	33	M	Tahlequah Dist	3351 Clifton roll
1869	1881		"	Nancy	32	F	" "	1220 Clifton roll
1870	1882		"	Rose	11	F	" "	1222 "
1871	1883		"	Clem	9	M	" "	1221 "
1872	1884		"	Fannie	7	F	" "	1223 "
1873	1885	379	Shepherd	Maria	32	F	" "	2055 b "
1874	1886	438	"	Ibby	10	F	" "	2056 b "
1875	1887		"	Willie	7	M	" "	2057 b
		Ill. Dist.						
1876	1888	388 John Dist	Smith	Bach	33	M	" "	2447 Clifton roll
1877	1889	272	"	Florence	20	F	" "	2,188 Formerly Pack
1878	1890		Sanders	Robert	30	M	" "	1321 Clifton roll
1879	1891		"	Mary	24	F	" "	
1880	1892		"	Allen	8	M	" "	1322 "
1881	1893	370	Schrimsher	Carrie	20	F	" "	1645 "
1882	1894	376	Shepherd	Susan	18/15	F	" "	1538 "
1883	1895	377	Sanders	Matilda	59	F	" "	
1884	1896	378	Sanders	Jennie	65	F	" "	
1885	1897	380	Sanders	Jim	20	M	" "	On Cher. roll "Fleming Sanders"
1886	1898	439	Smith	Isabella	22	F	" "	
		Ill. Dist.						
1887	1899	390	Smith	Alexander	23	M	" "	2445 Clifton roll

Authenticated Freedmen

Office No	Dawes Roll No	Cherokee No Tab Book	Names		age	Sex	Residence	
1888	1900	336	Saunders	Robert	32	M	Tahlequah Dist	
1889	1901	337	Smith	Jim	50	M	" "	Aged 50 on Chers roll of 1880 1087 Clifton roll
1890	1902	338	"	Tenah	40	F	" "	Age 40 on Cherokee roll of 1880 1088 Clifton roll
1891	1903	340	Sofkee	Minta	35	F	" "	
1892	1904	341	"	William	16	M	" "	
1893	1905	342	"	Lewis	14	M	" "	
1894	1906	344	Sanders	Ben	35	M	" "	1962 Clifton roll
1895	1907	345	Sanders	Simon	74	M	" "	
1896	1908	346	"	Sarah	59	F	" "	2159 "
1897	1909	348	"	Anderson	21	M	" "	2100 "
1898	1910	349	"	Harriet	16	F	" "	2097 "
1899	1911	347	Sanders	Ben	24	M	" "	2408 "
1900	1912	355	Sanders	Andrew	57	M	" "	
1901	1913	358	"	Alex	20	M	" "	
1902	1914	357	"	William	16	M	" "	
1903	1915	361	Shepherd	Thomas	21	M	" "	955 Clifton Roll
1904	1916	363	Shepherd	Lucinda	18	F	" "	1674 "

Authenticated Freedmen

Office No	Dawes Roll No	Choctaw No Nat Dist	Names		age	Sex	Residence		
1905	1917	368	Schrimsher	Fred	56	M	Tahlequah Dist		1643 Clifton roll
1906	1918	369	"	Sophia	52	F	"	"	1644 "
1907	1919	371	"	William	28	M	"	"	1647 "
1908	1920	342	"	Mary	16	F	"	"	1648 "
1909	1921	373	"	Jane	14	F	"	"	1480 "
1910	1922	374	"	Samantha	12	F	"	"	1650 "
1911	1923	391	Taylor	Vic	30	F	"	"	
1912	1924	393	Taylor	William	40	M	"	"	
1913	1925	394	"	Cora Ann	15	F	"	"	
1914	1926	390	Thompson	Will	30	M	"	"	1184 Clifton roll
1915	1927	91	"	Vic	28	F	"	"	1285 formerly Daniels
1916	1928	92	Daniels	Eli	11	M	"	"	
1917	1929		Johnson	Lizzie	8	F	"	"	
1918	1930		Thompson	Stephen	7	M	"	"	1186 Arkansas
1919	1931	255	Thompson	Flora	20	F	"	"	931 Clifton roll formerly Nivens
1920	1932	331	Thompson	Sarah	24	F	"	"	1430 formerly Riley
1921	1933	382	Thompson	Bart	50	M	"	"	1141 Clifton roll
1922	1934	384	"	William	17	M	"	"	1149 "
1923	1935	385	"	Annie	13	F	"	"	
1924	1936	386	"	Simon	14	M	"	"	
1925	1937	387	"	Carrie	11	F	"	"	
1926	1938		Thompson	Jonas	22	M	"	"	2099 "

Authenticated Freedmen

Office No.	Enrollment No.	Church No.	Names		age	sex	Residence	
		Saline Dist						
1924	1939	104	Vann	David	39	M	Tahlequah Dist	797 Clifton roll
1926	1940	105	"	Sarah	31	F	" "	748 "
1929	1941	107	"	Layman	11	M	" "	On Cher. roll "Lamon"
1930	1942		"	Robert	10	M	" "	800
1931	1943		"	Bertha A.	7	F	" "	801
		Ill Dist						
1932	1944	485	Vann	Daniel	55	M	" "	On Cher. roll "David"
1933	1945	486	"	Lottie	44	F	" "	1523 Clifton roll
1934	1946	455 493	"	Hannah George	18 a/o 1416	F	" "	On Cher. roll Julia
1935	1947	494	"	Jesse	17	M	" "	
1936	1948	495	"	Delila	14	F	" "	1507 Clifton roll
1937	1949	496	"	Esther	11	F	" "	1026 Clifton roll
1938		411	Jally	Aggie	90	F	" "	
		Saline Dist						
1939	1950	96	Vann	Kirk	51	M	" "	
1940	1951	97	"	Clora	44	F	" "	
1941	1952	99	"	Jane	18	F	" "	
1942	1953	100	"	Andy	17	M	" "	7030 "
1943	1954	101	"	Caroline	14	F	" "	
1944	1955	102	"	Ave	11	M	" "	
1945	1956	98	Vann	James	23	M	" "	7029 "
		Sal. Dist						
1946	1957	401	Vann	Charles	21	M	" "	1171 Clifton roll
1947	1958	287	Vann	Ann	28	F	" "	Formerly Ross
1948	1959		Ross	Hannah	9	F	" "	
1949	1960	440	Webber	George	14	M	"	Grandson of El Campbell
1950	1961	415	"	Lizzie	16	F	"	2108 Clifton wife of Ben Sanders

Authenticated Freedmen

			Names		age	Sex	Residence	
1957	1962	John Dist. 430(a)	Wilson	Henry	23	M	Tahlequah Dist	2168 Clifton roll. On cher. roll thick
1952	1963	430(b)	Williams	Dave	36	M	" "	M 59 Clifton roll
1953	1964	427	Wilson	Kate	39	F	" "	2199 "
1954	1965		"	Cora	8	F	" "	2200 "
1955	1966	Ill Dist. 59f	Williams	Lizzie	27	F	" "	
1956	1967		"	Henry	8	M	" "	
1957	1968	423	Wilson	Isaac	48	M	" "	1113 Clifton roll
1958	1969	424	"	Rachel	38	F	" "	1114 "
1959	1970	425	"	Becky	12	F	" "	1115 "
1960	1971	426	"	Peggy	10	F	" "	1116 "
1961	1972		"	Fred D.	7	M	" "	1117 "
1962	1973	416	Wilson	Sarah	34	F	" "	1252 "
1963	1974	417	"	Reed	11	M	" "	1253 "
1964	1975		"	Lelia	9	F	" "	1257 "
1965	1976		"	Thomas	7	M	" "	1258 "
1966	1977	408	Webber	Sam	39	M	" "	1683 "
1967	1978	409	"	Julia	37	F	" "	1684 "
1968	1979	410	"	Levi	17	M	" "	1672 "
1969	1980	411	"	Mary	14	F	" "	
1970	1981	412	"	Rosella	12	F	" "	780 Clifton roll
1971	1982		"	Frank	8	M	" "	
1972	1983		Watie	Joseph		M	" "	Dup. See 1432. See 14291 (91)

Authenticated Freedmen — Dead Roll

Office No	Wallace No	Columbus No	Names		Age	Sex	Residence		
1973	1984		Wofford	Sam	57	M	Tahlequah Dist.	2008	Clifton roll
1974	1985		"	Joseph	39	M	" "		"
1975	1986		"	Napoleon	21	M	" "	2009	"
1976	1987		"	Alma	18	F	" "	2810	"
1977	1988		"	George	16	M	" "		"
1978	1989		"	Melzy	14	F	" "	2011	"
1979	1990		"	Walter	12	M	" "	2012	"
1980	1991		"	Edward	10	M	" "	2013	"
1981	1992		"	James	8	M	" "	2014	"
1982	1993		Williams	Peter	80	M	" "	261 Clifton roll	
1983	1994		"	Judy	75	F	" "	262 Clifton roll	
1984	1995		Rowe	Rosie	36	F	" "	"	
1985	1996		"	Perry	16	M	" "	"	
1986	1997		"	Celia	14	F	" "	"	
1987	1998		Williams	Amanda	11	F	" "	"	
1988	1999		"	Joanna	24	F	" "	No 20 on Clifton roll	

1999
16
1973

Dead Roll

Office No	No	Tah. Dist.	Names		Age	Sex	Residence	Died	
1989	1	10	Baldridge	Silvia	64	F	Tahlequah Dist.	1884	
1990	2	17	Buffington	Henry	69	M	" "	June 1883	
1991	3	20	"	Helen	22	F	" "	1885	
1992	4	25	Brown	Joseph	23	M	" "	1886	
1993	5	26	Buffington	Charles	30	M	" "	1888	
1994	6	32	Bick	Walter	18	M	" "	1889	
1995	7	54	Campbell	Charlotte	66	F	" "	1885	
1996	8	57	"	Dilsey	92	F	" "	1885	
1997	9	82	Collins	Reuben	56	M	" "	1889	
1998	10	58	Evans	Feeling	48	M	" "	1887	

Authenticated Freedmen — Dead Roll

		Tahlequah Dist	Names		age	Sx	Residence	Died	
1999	11	133	Gentry	John	61	M	Tahlequah Dist	1886	
2000	12	151	Humphries	Nancy	32	F	" "	1889	2708 Clifton roll
2001	13	167	Harlin	Lucy Ann	40	F	" "	1887	
2002	14	183	Irns	Willie	15	M	" "	1888	
2003	15	193	Johnson	Willie	5	M	" "	1885	
2004	16	197	"	Katie	4	F	" "	1884	
2005	17	211	Lowery	Jesse	70	M	" "	1885	
2006	18	212	"	Cornelius	16	M	" "	1885	
2007	19	239	Mayes	Mary	47	F	" "	1887	
2008	20	270	Pack	Jack	61	M	" "	1885	
2009	21	294	Ross	Martha Jane	17	F	" "	1888	
2010	22	298	"	Harriet	49	F	" "	Nov. 1885	
2011	23	327	Rogers	Maggie	26	F	" "	1885	
2012	24	375	Schrimsher	Annie	74	F	" "	1884	
2013	25	Ill Dist 36	Brown	Henry	18	M	Illinois District	1886	
2014	26	57	Craps	Isaac	44	M	" "	1884	
2015	27	58	"	Louisa	45	F	" "	1885 after Mar.	
2016	28	91	"	Nancy	34	F	" "	1883	
2017	29	110	Coody	Joseph	17	M	" "	1888	
2018	30	127	Davis	Hayes	9	M	" "	1886	
2019	31	129	"	Ellen	76 4/0	F	" "	1886	
2020	32	136	Drew	Maria	17	F	" "	1889	
2021	33	151	Foreman	Fred	65	M	" "	1884	
2022	34	159	Fields	Henrietta	26	F	" "	1889	Cher. roll give age as 6 in 1880
2023	35	160	"	Minerva	24	F	" "	1889 after Mar.	" " " - 4 - "
2024	36	177	Foreman	Katie	14	F	" "	1883 after Mar.	
2025	37	179	"	Rogers	6	M	" "	1883	
2026	38	199	Glass	Rachel	29	F	" "	1886	
2027	39	231	Lewis	Nellie	26	F	" "	1889	per Jake Lewis adm.
2028	40	260	Mackey	Rachel	14	F	" "	1884	

Authenticated Freedmen — Dead Roll

No.			Names		Age	Sex	Residence	Died	
2029	41	261	Mackey	Jack	26	M	Illinois Dist	1888	died Chinguire age as 7 in 1880
2030	42	273	"	Lewis	36	M	" "	1886	
2031	44	252	Mayfield	Matthew	23	M	" "	1885	died Chinguire age as 8 in 1880
2032	45	286	Nave	Katie	59	F	" "	1889 after Man	
2033	46	290	Nevins	Louisa	43	F	" "	1883 after Man	
2034	47	295	"	Sarah	7	F	" "	1883	
2035	48	298	Pinder	Daniel	65	M	" "	1886	
2036	49	308	Parks	Mary	19	F	" "	1887	
2037	50	312	Payne	Percy	11	M	" "	1888	
2038	51	313	"	William	8	M	" "	1884	
2039	52	321	Ross	Carrie	8	F	" "	1885	
2040	53	329	"	Austin	26	M	" "	1883 after Man	
2041	54	339	Roach	Patsey	59	F	" "	1889	
2042	55	345	"	Nancy	32	F	" "	1887	
2043	56	367	Smith	Stephen	40	M	" "	1885 after Man	
2044	57	368	"	Nan	25	F	" "	1883	
2045	58	369	"	Cynthia	14	F	" "	1886	
2046	59	377	Sanders	Jack	26	M	" "	1884 after Man	
2047	60	378	"	Winnie	28	F	" "	1883	
2048	61	446	Theodore	Thomas	19	M	" "	1887	
2049	62	449	Thompson	Mums	75	M	" "	1885	
2050	63	450	"	Sarah	44	F	" "	1884	
2051	64	451	"	Isaac	30	M	" "	1887	
2052	65	453	Vann	Russell	68	M	" "	1889	
2053	66	455	"	Gracey	15	F	" "	1886	
2054	67	459	"	Ellis	20	M	" "	1884	
2055	68	471	"	Maria	45	F	" "	1885 after Man	
2056	69	483	"	Peggy	53	F	" "	1883	
2057	70	518	"	Cynthia	68	F	" "	1888	
2058	71	539	Walker	J. P. Boon	29	M	" "	1886	See # 28668 (93)

Authenticated Freedmen — Dead Roll

Office No.	Am. Bush No.	Census No.	Names		age	Sex	Residence	died	
		Ill. Dist.							
2059	72	600	Woodard	Harriet	34	F	Illinois Dist.	1885	
2060	73	601	"	James	13	M	" "	1885	
2061	74	603	"	Susan	66	F	" "	1886	
		Can Dist.							
2062	75	35	Brown	Joe	21	M	Cooweeskoowa Dist	1885	
2063	76	46	Chouteau	Robert	32	M	" "	1886	
2064	77	140	Lasley	Susan	68	F	" "	1888	
2065	78	161	Melton	Billy	71	M	" "	1886	
2066	79	162	"	Sallie	71	F	" "	1886	
2067	80	163	"	Sam	12	M	" "	1886	
2068	81	188	Nave	Wesley	24	M	" "	1889	
2069	82	276	Ross	Susan	44	F	" "	1885	
2070	83	370	Vann	Dave	33	M	" "	1884	
2071	84	402	Whitmire	Moses	40	M	" "	1884	Chero roll gives age as 30 in 1880
2072	85	404	"	Johnson	23	M	" "	1885	
2073	86	435	"	Moses	28	M	" "	1886	
2074	87	436	"	Nelson	26	M	" "	1885	Chero roll gives age as 16 in 1880
2075	88	437	"	Elbert	21	F	" "	1887	Should be Allen M.
		Can Dist							
2076	89	18	Drew	Katie	60	F	Canadian Dist	1885	
2077	90	51	Snow	Swim	16	M	" "	1889	
2078	91	53	"	Henry	11	M	" "	1888	
		Co. Sg. Dist							
2079	92	1	Alberty	Nicey	59	F	Going Snake Dist	1883	
		Flint Dist							
2080	93	5	Johnson	John	41	M	Flint Dist.	1886	
		Sal. Dist.							
2081	94	18	Bryant	Nancy	54	F	Saline Dist.	1886	
2082	95	32	Daniels	Celia	92	F	" "	1887	See # 15122 (92)
2083	96	33	Dickson	Jack	98	M	" "	1887	
2084	97	61	Lynch	Nancy	52	F	" "	1885	
2085	98	92	Sutton	Lewis	26	M	" "	1885	Born D 0876 See official — Bennett's Rolls no 78
2086	99	50	Johnson	George	44	M	" "	1884	Should be Redd Jernon
		Del. Dist.							
2087	100	20	Foster	Anika	41	F	Delaware Dist.	1887	Chero roll gives age as 31 in 1880
2088	101	32	Martin	Frederick	50	M	" "	1888	" " 50 , 1880

Authenticated Freedmen — Dead Roll

Office no.	Rollen no.	Census no.	Names		age	Sx	Residence		
2089	102	18	Depy	Walter	20	M	Sequoyah Dist.	1888	
2090	103	32	Johnson	Moses	75	M	" "	1888	
2091	104	37	"	Moses Jr.	12	M	" "	1889	
2092	105	41	"	Hester	38	F	" "	1883	on census roll as 33 in 1880
2093	106	55	"	Ellen	34	F	" "	1888	" " " 24 1880
2094	107	78	Wilton	Peggy	25	F	" "	1885	" " " 15 1880
2095	108	108	Wright	Ellen	28	F	" "	1890	

Admitted Freedmen

Office No.	Roll No.	Names		age	Sex	Residence	
	1	See "questioned list"					
2096	3	Adair	Henry	65	M	Delaware Dist.	
2097	4	Albert	Mattie	47	F	Sequoyah Dist.	3932 Clifton roll
2098	5	"	Nancy	20	F	" "	3934 "
2099	6	"	Henry	18	M	" "	3927 "
2100	7	"	Jerry	16	M	" "	3926 "
2101	8	"	Lillie	12	F	" "	3923 "
2102	9	"	Elijah	8	M	" "	3924 "
2103	10	Allen	Martha	60	F	" "	
2104	11	Adams	Perry	30	M	Cooweescoowee Dist	
2105	12	"	Eddie	9	M	" "	
2106	13	Alberty	Andrew	34	M	" "	3695 Clifton roll
2107	14	Adams	Katie	24	F	" "	4171 "
2108	15	Allen	Rose	37	F	" "	2540 Clifton roll
2109	16	"	William	13	M	" "	2541 "
2110	17	"	Annie	11	F	" "	2542 "
2111	18	"	George	8	M	" "	2544 "
	19	See "questioned list"					

Admitted Freedmen

No.	Letter	Names		age	sex	Residence			
2112	20	Beck	Maryland	43	M	Illinois Dist	3383	Clifton re'd
2113	21	McDanis	Lotta	20	F	" "	3384	"
2114	22	Beck	William	18	M	" "	Dead	
2115	23	"	Emeline	15	F	" "		
2116	24	"	Benjamin	13	M	" "	3385	"
2117	25	"	Dallas	11	M	" "	3386	
2118	26	"	Sara	9	F	" "	3387	"
2119	27	Ballard	Jennie	30	F	Going Snake Dist		
2120	28	Blade	Wm	14	M			
2121	29	"	Lena	11	F	" "		
2122	30	Ballard	Malcolm	7	M	" "		
2123	31	Buffington	Wm	22	M	Saline Dist		
2124	32	Bean	Mary	98	F	Delaware Dist		
2125	33	Brown	Ella	17	F	Cherokee Nation	See 164 2959 Clifton
2126	34	"	Lewis	16	M	" "	" 165 2958 "
2127	36	Brakebill	Louisa B	6	F	Delaware Dist	Born after Mar. 3.1883 #14291 (91) See that Louisa was born before March
2128	37	"	John J.	30	M	" "	3. 1883. (Born Feb. 14. 1885
2129	38	Barnes	Jennie	46	F	Going Snake Dist		
2130	39	"	Robert	21	M	" "		
2131	40	"	Sarah	19	F	" "		
2132	41	"	Maggie	17	F	" "		
2133	42	"	John	13	M	" "		
2134	43	"	Joshua	11	M	" "		
2135	44	"	Samuel	7	M	" "		

Admitted Freedmen

Office No.	Ration No.	Names		age	sex	Residence		
2136	45	Barnes	Low	25	F	Going Snake Dist.		
2137	46	French	Frank	12	M	" " "		
2138	47	Bargaman	Lizzie	18	F	Sequoyah Dist.		
2139	48	Brown	Susan	33	F	Canadian Dist.	2691	Clifton call
2140	49	Barden	Oscar	25	F	Sequoyah Dist.		
2141	50	Bryant	George	50	M	Saline Dist.	3513	,
2142	51	"	Rose	14	F	" "		
2143	52	Bean	Jacob	40	M	" "	4152	,
2144	53	Blackhawk	Steven	27	M	Sequoyah Dist.		
2145	54	Bean	Joseph	42	M	Saline Dist.		
2146	55	Burns	Robt.	54	M	Sequoyah Dist.		
2147	56	Bell	Thomas	52	M	" "		
2148	57	"	Harliner	44	F	" "		
	58	See "questioned list"						
	59	" " "						
	60	" " "						
	61	" " "						
2149	62	Black Hawk	Nancy	27	F	Sequoyah Dist.		
2150	63	Williams	Sampson	7	M	" "		

Admitted Freedmen

Office No.	Rolland No.	Names		age	sex	Residence	
2151	64	Bailey	Daisy	19	F	Muscogee	
2152	65	Bean	Cueby	75	F	Tahlequah Dist	
2153	66	"	Seraphine	16	F		
2154	67	Bean	Anderson	46	M	Tahlequah Dist	
2155	68	Bonie	Mary	32	F	Creek Nation	
2156	69	Briggs	Amanda	24	F	Tahlequah Dist	
2157	70	Brown	Mary	21	F	" "	
2158	71	Buffington	Alice	20	F	Creek Nation	
2159	72	Buffington	Mary	20	F	" "	
2160	73	Bean	Joseph	25	M	Tahlequah Dist	
	74	See "questioned list"					
2161	75	Buffington	Dosie	23	M	Illinois Dist	
2162	76	Buffington	Henry	23	M	Illinois Dist	No 5 Clifton will
2163	77	Brown	Jeff	52	M	" "	7777 "
2164	78	Brown	Jennie	25	F	Illinois Dist	formerly Crosland
2165	79	"	Elias	10	M	" "	
2166	80	"	David	9	M	" "	
2167	81	"	Lewis	8	M	" "	

Admitted Freedmen.

Office 83a	Wallace No.		Names		age	sex	Residence		
2168	82		Brewer	Samuel	69	M	Illinois Dist		see 4264 Clifton Roll
2169	83		"	Alonzo	17	M	"	"	
2170	84		"	Aurelia	15	F	"	"	
2171	85		"	George W.	11	M	"	"	
2172	86		Brown	John H.	24	M	Cooweeskoowa Dist		
2173	87		Bean	Arthur	44	M	"	"	2810 Clifton roll
2174	88	84	"	Alice	18	F	"	"	427 Clifton roll same as 568, see 4291 (91)
	89								
	90		See "questioned list"						
	91								
2175	92		Bryant	Ephraim	50	M	Cooweeskoowa Dist	4770½ Clifton roll	
2176	93		"	Minta	13	F	"	"	2772½ "
2177	94		"	Sherman	10	M	"	"	2773½ "
2178	95		"	Bertha	7	F	"	"	2774½ "
2179	96		Baldridge	Mary	19	F	"	"	
2180	97		Ball	Abby	39	F	"	"	3418 "
2181	98		Brown	George	52	M	"	"	
2182	99		"	Amanda	53	F	"	"	
2183	100		"	Carrie	22	F	"	"	
2184	101		"	John	20	M	"	"	
2185	102		"	Wm	12	M	"	"	

Admitted Freedmen

Office No	Rolls No	Names		age	Sex	Residence		
2186	103	Beck	Helens	35	M	Coonaskoonu Dist		
2187	104	"	Minnie	36	F	"	"	
2188	105	"	Charlotte	13	F	"	"	"
2189	106	"	Ida	9	F	"	"	
2190	107	"	Annie	8	F	"	"	
2191	108	"	Fannie	8	F	"	"	
2192	109	"	James	7	M	"	"	
2193	110	Binckley	Lizzie	35	F	"	"	
2194	111	"	Horace	8	M	"	"	
2195	112	Buffington	Ab.	24	M	"	"	
2196	113	"	Eliza	14	F	"	"	
2197	114	Brown	Ettie	26	F	"	"	
2198	115	"	Richard	13	M	"	"	
2199	116	"	George	10	M	"	"	
2200	117	"	Owen	8	M	"	"	
2201	118	"	Cindy	6	F	"	"	Born after Mar. 3-63 14291 (91) 7031 (91)
2202	119	Bell	George	29	M	"	"	Filed certif. of Ex. Dept Cher. Nation for birth —
2203	120	"	July	32	M	"	"	alias J. Armistead
2204	121	Brown	Charles	59	M	"	"	
2205	122	"	Charles Jr.	19	M	"	"	
2206	123	"	Samuel	17	M	"	"	
2207	124	"	Washington	15	M	"	"	
2208	125	"	Luvinia	10	F	"	"	
2209	126	"	Joseph	7	M	"	"	

Admitted Freedmen

Office No	Roll No	Names		age	Sex	Residence			
2210	127	Bean	Henry	40	M	Canceekonee Dist			
2211	128	Sidney	Lucinda	12	F	"	"		
2212	129	Bean	Tobias	50	M	"	"	3910	Clifton roll
2213	130	"	Caroline	12	F	"	"	3911	"
2214	131	"	Arthur	10	M	"	"	3912	"
2215	132	Bean	John	48	M	"	"		
	133	See "questioned list"							
2216	134	Bean	Emma	28	F	"	"		
2217	135	"	John H	19	M	"	"		
2218	136	"	Flora	17	F	"	"		
2219	137	"	Andrew	16	M	"	"	3651	Clifton roll
2220	138	"	Lucinda	15	F	"	"		
2221	139	"	Eliza	13	F	"	"		
2222	140	"	Ebby	10	F	"	"		
2223	141	"	Sandy	9	M	"	"	3652	"
2224	142	"	Lottie	7	F	"	"	3653	"
2225	143	Buffington	Amanda	8	F	"	"		
2226	144	"	Nelson	7	M	"	"		
2227	145	Bean	Rachel	77	F	"	"	3197	Clifton roll
2228	146	"	Mary	14	F	"	"	3199	"
2229	147	"	Lucy	9	F	"	"	3200	"
2230	148	"	Margaret	9	F	"	"		
2231	149	Beck	Samuel	45	M	"	"		
		Why is wife not enrolled?							

Admitted Freedmen

Office No	Dawes No	Names		age	sex	Residence		
2232	150	Baldridge	John	55	M	Cooweescoowee Dist	3142	Clifton roll
2233	151	"	Ellen	28	F	"	"	
2234	152	"	John Jr	19	M	"	3144	"
2235	153	"	andelew Jackson	18	M	"	3145	"
2236	154	"	Columbus	15	M	"	3146	"
2237	155	Buckner	Sarah C	33	F	"	2512	Clifton roll
2238	156	"	Ella	16	F	"	2513	"
2239	157	"	Arthur	8	M	"	2514	"
2240	158	"	Bessie	7	F	"	"	
2241	159	Bean	Leander	38	M	"	2839	"
2242	160	Blackburn	Charles	37	M	"	2882	"
	161	See "questioned list"						
2243	162	Blackburn	Nora	7	F	"	2286	"
2244	163	"	John O'Niel	9	M	"	2885	"
2245	164	Ballard	Polly	65	F	"	"	
2246	165	Foreman	Mattie	10	F	"		
2247	166	Bell	Matilda	21	F	"		
2248	167	"	Maria	19	F	"		
2249	168	"	Peter	14	M	"	claims to be 18 + same his living	
2250	169	"	John	12	M	"		
2251	170	Bowles	Emma	22	F	"	3849 Clifton roll	
						child of 479 Cooweescoowee Dist		
3252	171	Campbell	Joe	34	M	Tahlequah Dist	2963 Clifton roll See that he is not same as no 726	
2253	172	Drew	Rachel	15	F		Auth. roll	

Admitted Freedmen

		Names		age	Sex	Residence	
2254	173	Childers	Caroline	70	F	Sequoyah Dist.	
2255	174	Chouteau	Louisa	60	F	Tahlequah Dist	2785 Clifton roll
2256	175	Chouteau	Mary	23	F	" "	2787 "
2257	176	"	William		M	" "	Born after Mar. 3 '83 # 4291 (91)
2258	177	Lewis	Richard	8	M	" "	
2259	178	Chambers	Sherman	21	M	Cherokee Nation	
2260	179	Colonel	Jane	51	F	Saline Dist.	
2261	180	Foster	John	21	M	" "	
2262	181	Vann	Daisey	8	F	" "	
2263	182	Childers	Rob	24	M	Illinois Dist.	
						" "	
	183	See questioned list					
2264	184	Chambers	Judy	60	F	Sequoyah Dist	
2265	185	Warren	Rufus	26	M	" "	
2266	186	West	David	14	M	" "	
2267	187	Denenburg	Clark	13	M	" "	
2268	188	Paden	Polly	11	F	" "	
2269	189	"	Dennis	7	M	" "	
2270	190	Carter	John	28	M	Delaware Dist	3689 Clifton roll
2271	191	"	Jerry	8	M	" "	3690
2272	192	Choate	Edward	40	M	Illinois Dist	2776 Clifton roll

Admitted Freedmen

Office No.	Wallace No.	Names		age	sex	Residence			
2273	194	Chouteau	Samuel	53	M	Tahlequah Dist	2786	Clifton roll	
2274	195	Carter	Ellis	19	M	Coowescoowee Dist	Jane Hare 242 Tel Dist		
2275	196	"	Anna	14	F	"	" " "		
2276	197	Campbell	Edmond	65	M	Tahlequah Dist			
2277	198	Chambers	Sabra	18	F	Coowescoowee Dist	No. 38 Coo. Dist. father		
2278	199	"	Wm	22	M	"	" "		
2279	200	"	Richard	14	M	"	"		
2280	201	Chouteau	Dido	14	F	"	"		
2281	202	Foggy	Jack	7	M	"	"		
2282	203	Campbell	Emma	37	F	"	"	2518	Clifton roll
2283	204	"	George	17	M	"	"	2519	"
2284	205	"	Jim	15	M	"	"	2520	"
2285	206	"	Walter	12	M	"	"	2521	"
2286	207	"	Charles	10	M	"	"		
2287	208	"	John	8	M	"	"	2522	"
2288	209	Campbell	Ed.	45	M	"	"	2614	"
2289	210	"	Mary	14	F	"	"	2613	"
2290	211	Coody	Susan	90	F	"	"	3871	"
	212	see questioned list							
2291	213	Cocoa	Bunke	55	M	"	"	2493	Clifton roll

Admitted Freedmen

Office No	Roll No		Names		age	sex	Residence	
2292	214		Carter	Sally	31	F	Ft. Smith ark.	3316 Clifton roll
2293	215		Coody	Jackson	27	M	Cooweeskoowee Dist	
2294	216		Carter	Robert	45	M	" "	Died Dec. 7, 1889, see No 15118 (92)
2295	217		"	Ella	7	F	" "	
2296	218	313	Coates	Sophronia	40	F	" "	Same as No. 63, see No 14291
	219		See questioned list					
2297	220		Colbert	James	29	M	" "	3616 Clifton roll
2298	221		Coody	Lewis	50	M	" "	4219 "
	222							
-	223							
	224		See questioned list					
	225							
	226							
	227							
2299	228		Claggett	Nancy	22	F	Cooweeskoowee Dist	
2300	229		Carter	Louisa	45	F	" "	
2301	230		Calender	Gertie	7	F	" "	Born after Mar. 3, '83 No 14291 (9). Born May 1883 No 14705 7 31 (91)
2302	231		Carver	Mary	28	F	" "	
2303	232		Riley	Parthenia	13	F	" "	
2304	233		Bryant	Birdie	7	F	" "	

Admitted Freedmen

Office No.	Roll No.	Names		age	sex	Residence		
2305	234	Cobbin	Melzey	35	F	Commuckhomee Dist		
2306	235	"	Wm	18	M	"	"	
2307	236	"	Nettie	16	F	"	"	
2308	237	"	James	14	M	"	"	
2309	238	"	Sandford	12	M	"	"	
2310	239	"	Lee	11	M	"	"	
2311	240	"	Matthew	9	M	"	"	
2312	241	"	Alexander	7	M	"	"	
2313	242	Chouteau	Dido	80	F	"	"	
	243	See questioned list						
	244	"	"	"				
2314	245	Daniels	Burrell	60	M	Creek Nation	4504	Clifton
2315	246	"	Miranda	61	F	"	"	
2316	247	"	Burrell Jr	18	M	"	"	4506	"
2317	248	"	Mack	16	M	"	"	4507	"
2318	249	"	Lizzie	14	F	"	"	4508	"
2319	250	"	Robert	12	M	"	"	4509	"
2320		"	Mary	10	F	"	"	4510	
2321	251	Newton	Lizzie	8	F	"	"	4511	
2322	252	Davis	Charles	43	M	Commuckhomee Dist		
2323	253	"	Lizzie	16	F	"	"	
2324	254	"	Emma	14	F	"	"	
2325	255	Duffin	Josh	35	M	"	"	

Admitted Freedmen

Office No	No	Names		age	sex	Residence			
2326	256	Durant	Peggie	39	F	Coweackawaa Dist	4116	Clifton roll	
2327	257	"	Eddie	20	M	" "	4117	"	
2328	258	"	Rosie	18	F	" "	4118	"	
2329	259	Davis	J D	38	M	" "			
2330	260	Drew	Jeannette	14	F	Illinois Dist	child of 134 Ill. Dist		
2331	261	Davis	Jackson	61	M	Delaware Dist	2528 Clifton roll husband of 2346		
2332	262	Daniels	Giles	70	M	Tahlequah Dist			
2333	263	Drew	Judy	65	F	Illinois Dist			
2334	264	Perkins	Walter	13	M	" "			
2335	265	Daniels	George	34	M	Delaware Dist	2812 Clifton roll		
2336	266	"	Moses	13	M	" "			
2337	267	"	Enoch	12	M	" "	2813 "		
2338	268	"	Cynthia	10	F	" "	2814 "		
2339	269	Downing	Elias	49	M	" "			
2340	270	"	Johnson	14	M	" "			
2341	271	"	Elizabeth	11	F	" "	2878 "		
2342	272	"	Mary L	7	F	" "			
2343	273	Daniels	Harriet	50	F	Coweackawaa Dist	3201 "		
2344	274	Duffin	Frances	61	F	" "			
2345	275	Duffin	George B.	36	M				

Admitted Freedmen

Office No.	Roll No.	Names		Age	Sex	Residence	
2346	276	Davis	Carrie	53	F	Delaware Dist	w 29 Clifton roll wife of 2331
2347	277	Davis	Joe	34	M	Cooweescoowee Dist	2840 "
2348	278	"	John	12	M	" "	2841 Clifton roll
2349	279	"	Jim	10	M	" "	2842 "
2350	280	"	Lizzie	7	F	" "	2843 "
2351	281	Daniels	Andrew	26	M	" "	
2352	282	"	William	7	M	" "	
2353	283	Daniels	Celia	43	F	Saline Dist	3778 "
2354	284	"	George	20	M	" "	3779 "
2355	285	"	Frank	18	M	" "	3780 "
2356	286	"	Eva	14	F	" "	3781 "
2357	287	"	Donald	10	M	" "	3782 "
2358	288	Dickson	Eliza	40	F	Cooweescoowee Dist	See 11805 93 for Eliza Ross
2359	289	Cooper	Thomas	16	M	"	Her says he is 19 years old & is remarried living same with mother see office 876
2360	290	Daniels	Andrew	50	M	Cherokee Nation	
2361	291	"	Abbie	36	F	" "	
2362	292	"	Charles	25	M	" "	3039 Clifton roll
2363	293	"	Thomas	19	M	" "	3042 "
2364	294	"	Lucinda	17	F	" "	3041 "
2365	295	"	Lewis	16	M	" "	
2366	296	"	Josephine	14	F	" "	3043 "
2367	297	"	Jonas	13	M	" "	3042 "
2368	298	Daniels	James H.	26	M	Cooweescoowee Dist	3037 "

Admitted Freedmen

			Names		age	♀	Residence	
2369	299	Adair	Davis	Wm	35	M	Cherokee Nation	953 Clifton road
2370	300	49?	"	Emma	35	F	" "	
2371	301		"	Joseph	7	M	" "	
	303		see questioned list					
2372	304		Eastman	Isaac	24/44	M	Cooweeskoowee Dist	2594 "
	315		see questioned list					
	316		" "					
	317		see questioned list					
	318		" " "					
2373	319		Fulsom	Jesse	22	M	" "	
	320		see questioned list					
2374	321		Foster	Willie	17	M	Cooweeskoowee Dist	
2375	322		"	Lizzie	15	F	" "	
2376	323		see questioned list					
2376	324		Fields	Hannah	56	F	Cooweeskoowee Dist	
2377	325		Foreman	Charity	80	F	" "	
2378	326		Foreman	Charles	48	M	Creek Nation	
2379	327		Foster	Olmstead	27	M	" "	

Admitted Freedmen

Office No.	Roll No.	Names		age	sex	Residence		
2380	328	French	Benjamin	38	M	Muscogee.		
2381	329	Freeman	John	55	M	Cooweeskoowee Dist	3016	Clifton roll
2382	330	"	Abe	13	M	" "	"	"
2383	331	"	Mary	11	F	" "	3025	"
2384	332	"	John H.	9	M	" "	3020	"
2385	333	"	Eleanor	7	F	" "	3021	"
2386	334	"	Nettie	50	F	" "		
2387	335	"	Eliza	20	F	" "	3018	"
2388	336	Fields	Katie	12	F	Tahlequah Dist	2114 Clifton roll Mother Ann Fields 452 Tahlequah	
2389	337	Fox	Elan	60	M	Cooweeskoowee Dist	2485	clifton roll
2390	338	"	Nancy	39	F	" "	2486	"
2391	339	"	Angeline	11	F	" "	2487	" "
2392	340	"	Eliza	6	F	" "	2488	" "
2393	341	Foreman	Jesse Rowe	80	M	Delaware Dist		
2394	342	"	Chaney	18	F	" "		
	343	See questioned list						
2395	344	Francis	Minerva	35	F	Cooweeskoowee Dist	3821	"
2396	345	"	Jack	13	M	" "	3823	"
2397	346	Francis	Emma	19	F	" "	3822	"
2398	347	Fosler	Robert	46	M	Delaware Dist		
2399	348	"	Meldra	11	F	" "		
2400	349	"	Lucy Jane	9	F	" "		

Admitted Freedmen

Office No	Dollar No	Names		age	Sex	Residence	
2401	351	Freeman	Mack	25	M	Conneehorree Dist	
2402	353	French	Jimmie	15	M	" "	3227 Clifton roll
2403	354	"	Martha	13	F	" "	
2404	355	"	Willie	11	M	" "	
2405	356	"	Emeline	8	F	" "	3228 "
2406	357	Gunter	Henry	19	M	Sequoyah Dist	2956 Clifton roll
2407	358	"	Isaac	16	M	" "	2957
2408	359	Scales	Mary	8	F	" "	
	360	See questioned list					
2409	361	Gibson	Sarah	22	F	Conneehorree Dist	by 51st Clifton Roll Formerly Wilson
2410	362	Gunter	Henry	54	8	" "	4025 Clifton
2411	363	"	Henrietta	8	F	" "	4026 "
	364) 365)	See questioned list					3954 Clifton roll
2412	366	Gaines	Eliza	50	F	Delaware Dist	Stow ? 35878 (91)
2413	367	Nash	Julia	25	F	" "	3955 Clifton roll
2414	368	"	Melinda J	20	F	" "	3959 "
2415	369	"	Eliza	14	F	" "	3990 "
2416	370	"	Manda M	13	F	" "	
2417	371	"	William	12	M	" "	
2418	372	"	Berry	11	M	" "	3961 "
2419	373	"	Eddie	10	M	" "	3962 "
2420	374	"	Isaac	8	M	" "	3963 "
	375	on Free list					

Admitted Freedmen

Office No.	Roller No.		Names	age	sex	Residence			
2421	376	Gibson	Lewis	39	M	Cherokee Nation	2502	Clifton roll	
2422	377	"	Napoleon B.	17	M	" "	2503	"
2423	378	"	Wm	15	M	" "	2504	"
2424	379	"	Rosanna	14	F	" "		
2425	380	"	Posey	12	F	" "		
2426	381	Graves	Rachel	30	F	Illinois Dist		
2427	382	"	Robert	12	M	" "		
2428	383	"	James	10	M	" "		
2429	385	Gunter	Maggie	20	F	Cooweescoowee Dist	4027	Clifton roll
2430	386	"	Lewis	14	M	" "	4028	"
2431	387	"	Bettie	12	F	" "	4029	"
2432	388	"	Mitchell	9	M	" "	4030	"
2433	389	"	Rachel	7	F	" "	4031	"
2434	390	Gaskell	Low	28	F	" "	3858	"
2435	391	"	Walter	9	M	" "	3859	"
2436	392	"	Joella	7	F	" "	3860	"
2437	393	Gales	Martha	36	F	Canadian Dist	2688	Clifton roll
2438	394	Gunter	John	27	M	Illinois Dist	2954	"
2439	396	Gunter	Frances	39	F	Sequoyah Dist		
2440	397	Wilson	Ephraim	17	M	" "		
2441	398	"	Peggy	13	F	" "		
2442	399a	"	Easter	11	F	" "		
2443	399-b	Henry	Lucy	19	F	Saline Dist		

Admitted Freedmen

Office No	Dollars No	Names		Age	Sex	Residence		
2444	400	Henson	James	30	M	Cherokee Nation		
2445	401	Haynes	Mary	35	F	Canadian Dist.	3347	Clifton roll
2446	402	"	Allen	11	M	" "	3347	"
2447	403	Harris	Anna	27	F	Delaware Dist.		
2448	404	Holt	Lou	18	F	Sequoyah Dist.	2953	Clifton roll
2449	405	Howell	Mary	34	F	Carthage Mo.		
2450	406	"	Hester A.E.	10	F	claim Sequoyah Dist		
2451	407	Harlin	Mary	25	F	Tahlequah Dist.		
2452	408	Hawkins	Mary	32	F	Cherokee Nation		
2453	409	Thompson	Eveline	12	F	"		
2454	410	Hill	Lina	39	F	Ft. Smith Ark.	3292	"
2455	411	"	Anna George	18	F	" " "	3293	"
2456	412	"	John W.	12	M	" " "	3294	"
2457	413	Humphrey	Sally	42	F	Caddo. Chick. Nat.	2653	Clifton roll
2458	414	Murrell	Mattie	18	F	" " "	2684	"
2459	415	Humphrey	Ada	8	F	" " "	2685	"
2460	416	"	Ida	8	F	" " "	2686	"

Admitted Freedmen

Office No.	Roll No.	Names		age	Sex	Residence	
2461	417	Hudson	Mary	55	F	Conneskonvee Dist	
2462	418	Beeson	Jonathan	22	M	" "	
2463	419	Whitmire	Elizabeth	20	F	" "	Dead
2464	420	Beeson	Wm	18	M	" "	
2465	421	"	Jesse	15	M	" "	
2466	422	Hopkins	Delia B.	18	F	" "	Formerly Vann
2467	423	Holt	Becky	33	F	" "	4045 Clifton roll
2468	424	"	Frank	17	M	" "	4046 "
2469	425	"	Bertha	14	F	" "	
2470	426	"	Nellie	11	F	" "	
2471	427	"	Elias	9	M	" "	
2472	428	"	Cora	8	F	" "	
2473	429	"	Rebecca	7	F	" "	
2474	430	Hughes	Charles	33	8	" "	3792 Clifton roll
2475	431	"	Walter	8	M	" "	3793 "
2476	432	Holt	Josh	39	M	Ft. Scott, Kansas	3620 Clifton roll
2477	433	"	Jane	20	F	" " "	Formerly Johnson
2478	434	"	Laura	7	F	" " "	3621 "
2479	435	Hickey	Peggy	50	F	Conneskonva Dist	3554 Clifton roll See 2d Payroll Nov 5 & 4 for 1891
	436	See questioned list					
2480	437	Hildebrand	Calvin	48	M	" "	3496 Clifton roll

Admitted Freedmen

Office No.	Dawes Roll No.	Names		age	sex	Residence		
2481	438	Hazelrigg	Mary W.	34	F	Cherokee Nation	4017	Clifton roll
2482	439	"	Wm A.	13	M	" "	4018	"
2483	440	"	Mary	8	F	" "	4019	"
2484	441	"	Jesse or Jessie	8	M?	" "	4020	"
2485	442	Hicks	Mary	35	F	Cooweescoowee Dist.		
2486	443	"	Joseph	16	M	" "	2931	Clifton roll
2487	444	"	James A	14	M	" "	2932	"
2488	445	"	Catherine	12	F	" "	2933	"
2489	446	"	Eliza	10	F	" "	2934	"
2490	447	"	Leroy	8	M	" "	2935	"
2491	448	Hight	Mary	52	F	Ft. Smith, Ark.	Daughter of Eben Bean	
2492	449	Hudson	Peter	60	M	Cooweescoowee Dist	3543	Clifton roll
2493	450	"	Wm	29	M	" "	3544	"
2494	453	Irons	George	26	M			
2495	454	Irons	Alexander	33	M	Illinois Dist.	2939½	Clifton roll
2496	455	Ives	Sadie	22	F	Delaware Dist	Descendant of Angeline Vratie	
2497	456	Johnson	Mary	90	F	Saline Dist.		
2498	457	Johnson	Easter	50	F	Sequoyah Dist.		
2499	458	Jenkins	George	28	M	Illinois Dist.	2632	Clifton roll

Admitted Freedmen

Office No	Roll No	Names		age	sex	Residence	
2500	459	Johnson	Isam	46	M	Sequoyah Dist	
2501	460	"	Josephine	13	F	" "	
2502	461	"	Clara Bell	11	F	" "	
2503	462	"	Paul	10	M	" "	
2504	463	"	Isaac	8	M	" "	
2505	464	Johnson	Anna	30	F	Saline Dist	(?) 1332 not the same ref q 3011 See X 14705
2506	465	Johnson	Cynthia	19	F	Sequoyah Dist	wife of 763 Wallace Auth list
2507	466	Jones	Aggie	40	F	Illinois Dist	wife of Henderson Jones
2508	467	Jackson	Ada	32	F	" "	
2509	469	Johnson	Reuben	40	M	Cherokee Nation	3478 Clifton roll
2510	470	"	Solomon	12	M	" "	3479 "
2511	471	"	Eliza	9	F	" "	"
2512	472	"	Rosanna	7	F	" "	3480 "
2513	473	James	Nancy	40	F	Canadian Dist	2657 Clifton roll
2514	474	"	Allen	14	M	" "	2660 "
2515	475	"	Arch	9	M	" "	2661 "
2516	476	"	Ben	7	M	" "	2662 "
2517	477	Johnson	Sarah J	22	F	Delaware Dist	
2518	478	Johnson	Amanda	30	F	Cherokee Nation	3486 wife of 469 above
2519	479	"	Mary	14	F		
2520	480	"	Ruthra	13	F		

Admitted Freedmen

No.	No.	Names		age	sx	Residence		
2521	481	Johnson	Walker	36	M	Cherokee Nation	3649	Clifton roll
2522	482	"	Henry	17	M	" "	"	"
2523	483	"	George	15	M	" "	"	"
2524	484	Jones	Sophia	34	F	Cooweeskoowee Dist		
2525	485	"	Anna	15	F	" "		
2526	486	"	Lulu	10	F	" "		
2527	487	Kimbo	Hannah	40	F	Delaware Dist		
2528	488	"	Mary Ann	8	F	" "		
	489	see question list						
2529	490	Kennard	Polly Ann	45	F	Cooweeskoowee Dist	2992	Clifton roll
2530	491	"	Lucie	16	F	" "	2993	"
2531	492	"	David	11	M	" "	2994	"
2532	493	"	Delia	7	F	" "	2995	"
2533	494	Kirk	Emory	58	M	" "	3217	"
2534	495	"	Eveline	59	F	" "	3218	"
2535	496	Keys	Eliza	30	F	" "	wife of 127 Cooweeskoowee Dist
2536	497	Keys	Lucinda	76	F	Illinois Dist		
2537	498	"	Alexander	20	M	" "	2729	Clifton roll
2538	499	Ross	David	13	M	" "		
	500	see question list						
2539	501	Keyes	Frank	27	M	Sequoyah Dist	2960	"
2540	503	Landrum	Feriby	17	F	Cooweeskoowee Dist		
2541	504	Landrum	Callie M.	36	M	Delaware Dist	2482	Clifton roll

Admitted Freedmen

Office No.	[Roll No.]	Names		age	sex	Residence	
2542	505	Landrum	Martha	28	F	Delaware Dist.	3645 Clifton roll
	507	See rejected list					See 2868 (91)
2543	508	Leak	Sim	7	M	Coowescoowee Dist	Child of 153 Coowescoowee Dist No. 154 on Wallace Addt. list
2544	509	Little	Agnes	23	F	" "	4067 Clifton roll
2545	510	Looney	Steve	48	M	" "	3515 Clifton roll
2546	511	"	Peggy	57	F	" "	3516 Formerly Ross "
2547	512	Lacy	Matilda	59	F	" "	Dead
2548	513	Lynch	Rachel	30	F	Delaware Dist.	
2549	514	Looney	Alfred	37	M	Coowescoowee Dist	3529 Clifton roll
	515	See rejected list					3537
2550	516	"	Alice	7	F	" "	Born Mch 3, 83 # 1429 (91)
2551	517	Lasley	John	28	M	Cherokee Nation	
	518-519-520	See rejected list					
2552	521	Lynch	Daniel	18	M	Saline Dist	3915 Clifton roll
2553	522	Lynch	Joseph	34	M	Coowescoowee Dist	3009½ Clifton roll
2554	523	"	George	13	M	" "	Died 3011½ Dup. 7 26/5 " See 1429 (91)
2555	524	"	Wm	9	M	" "	3010½ "

Admitted Freedmen

H. no.	Roll no.	Names		age	sex	Residence	
2556	526	Leak	Edward	75	M	Cherokee Nation	2405 Clifton roll
2557	527	"	Allen	29	M	" "	Dup. same as 153
2558	528	"	Edward Jr	23	M	" "	2406 Clifton roll
2559	529	"	Henry	19	M	" "	2407 " "
2560	530	"	Eliza	11	F	" "	
2561	531	"	Steven	7	M	" "	
2562	532	"	Elizabeth	49	F	" "	2408 Clifton roll. wife of 526. See 2556
2563	533	Lowrey	Tobe	60	M	" "	
2564	534	"	Jacob	25	M	" "	3530 Clifton roll
2565	535	"	Frank	16	M	" "	3531 "
2566	536	Leak	Marilla	36	F	" "	wife of 528
2567	537	Chambers	Grant	20	M	" "	" "
2568	538	Ross	Henry	18	M	" "	
2569	539	Vann	Jesse	10	M	" "	
2570	540	Landrum	Arch	45	M	Delaware Dist	2851 Clifton roll
2571	541	Lowrey	Jess	32	M	Illinois Dist	3286 "
2572	544	Lynch	George W	38	M	Delaware Dist	3012 "
2573	545	"	Rosetta	7	F	" "	3013 "
2574	546	Lowrey	Josh	40	M	Tahlequah Dist.	4438 "

Admitted Freedmen

Mil. No.	Ded. No.	Names		age	sex	Residence	
2575	547	Lane	Rachel	48	F	Delaware Dist.	
2576	548	"	Wm	20	M	"	"
2577	549	"	Reuben	19	M	"	"
2578	550	"	Ira	17	M	"	"
2579	551	"	Lotta	15	F	"	"
2580	552	"	Zed	13	M	"	"
2581	553	"	Mitchell	10	M	"	"
2582	554	"	Anna	9	F	"	"
2583	555	"	Laura	8	F	"	"
2584	556	Lynch	Joseph	50	M	"	"
2585	557	"	Sophia	35	F	"	"
2586	558	"	Hester	19	F	"	"
2587	559	"	Nancy	17	F	"	"
2588	560	"	Martha	16	F	"	"
2589	561	"	Wm	15	M	"	"
2590	562	"	Cyrus	14	M	"	"
2591	563	"	Hayes	11	M	"	"
2592	564	"	John	10	M	"	"
2593	565	"	Arthur	9	M	"	"
2594	566	"	Rachel	8	F	"	"
2595	567	"	Vina	7	F	"	"
2596	568	Landrum	Charles	21	M	"	" See 2d pay roll remks 3-4 9ɥ 1871. Not satisfactorily identified 4291 (91) daughter of Jennie McNair no 644
2597	569	Lane	George Helen	12	M	Cooweskowee Dist.	
2598	570	"	James A.G.	9	M	"	"

Admitted Freedmen

Office No.	Collin No.	Names		age	Sex	Residence			
2599	571	McNair	Laura E.	16	F	Conweeskmore Dist			
2600	572	"	Isabella	14	F	" "			
2601	573	"	Sarah	11	F	" "		Grandchildren of 554 Cos. Dist	
2602	574	"	Flora	9	F	" "			
2603	575	Martin	Charles	40	M	" "	3391	Clifton roll	
2604	576	"	Mary Emma	15	F	" "	3393	"	
2605	577	"	Mazella	12	F	" "			
2606	578	"	Edna	9	F	" "	3395	"	
	579	See Questioned list							
2607	580	Martin	Jobe	40	M	Delaware Dist	3514	"	
2608	581 582	" See Questioned list	Nathan	14	M	" "			
2609	583	Mayes	Wm	23	M	Saline Dist			
2610	584	McClain	Joseph	53	M	" "	3569	"	
2611	589	Melton	Peter	13	M	Conweeskmore Dist			
2612	590	"	Ellen	10	F	" "			
2613	591	Martin	Arthur	19	M	Delaware Dist			
2614	592	"	Joseph	14	M	" "			Dead
2615	593	"	Wm	12	M	" "	Children of 585 Wallace's		"
2616	594	"	John	10	M	" "	auth list		"
	595	See Questioned list							
2617	596	Melton	Peggy	32	F	Conweeskmore Dist	3011 ½	Clifton roll	
2618	597	"	George	15	M	" "	See № 2554		
2619	598	"	Henry	10	M	" "			
2620	599	Martin	July (Julius?)	30	M	" "	3991	Clifton roll	

Admitted Freedmen

Ch'kee No.	Dawes No.	Names		age	Sex	Residence	
2621	600	Morgan	Rachel	34	F	Cooweeskoowee Dist	
2622	601	Martin	James	35	M	Delaware Dist	
2623	602	Milton	Phebe	36	F	" "	7940 Clifton roll
2624	603	"	Maud M.	15	F	" "	7941 "
2625	604	"	Willie	13	M	" "	
2626	605	"	Rose	10	F	" "	7943 "
2627	606	"	Josie	8	F	" "	7944 "
2628	607	McNair	Columbus	39	M	" "	7850 Clifton roll
2629	608	Musgrove	Minnow	22	M	Illinois Dist	son of Rat. Rogers 2106 o Dist
2630	609	McAuwa	Emma	18	F	" "	3287 Clifton roll C Granddaughter of Jack Brown Ill Dist
2631	610	Mackey	Roswell	34	M	Creek Nation	son of Malinda Smith 372 Ill Dist
2632	611	Mayes	Josh	32	M	Tahlequah Dist	3340 Clifton roll
2633	612	Starr	Barbary	64	F	" "	
2634	613	Mayfield	Lizzie	20	F	Sequoyah Dist	child of Francis Hunter 396 admitted list
2635	614	Mayfield	Charles	25	M	" "	child of Francis Hunter 396 Admitted list
2636	615	Meigs	Lucinda McL	37	F	Cherokee Nation	
2637	616	"	Irene	7	F	" "	
2638	617	Manley	Joseph	23	M	" "	3591 Clifton roll

Admitted Freedmen

Office No.	Indian No.	Names		Age	Sex	Residence		
2639	618	McNair	Jesse	32	M	Conwaskoowee Dist	4206	Clifton roll
2640	620	McDonald	John	40	M	Sequoyah Dist		
2641	621	"	John Jr	11	M	"	"	
2642	622	Mayfield	Phebe	55	F	"	"	
2643	623	Miller	Fannie	32	F	Conweekoowee Dist	Daughter of Maria McNair	
2644	624	Martin	Wm	28	M	"	"	2497 Clifton
2645	625	Martin	Helen	64	M	"	"	3120 "
2646	626	"	Rachel	50	F	"	"	3149 "
2647	627	"	Arthur	18	M	"	"	3128
2648	628	"	James	17	M	"	"	181 Clifton roll
2649	629	"	Harvey	15	M	"	"	3127 "
2650	630	"	Wm E.	15	M	"	"	3123 "
2651	631	"	Luther	14	M	"	"	3138 "
2652	632	"	Joseph	10	M	"	"	3125 "
2653	633	"	Jerry	8	M	"	"	3126 "
2654	634	Moore	Mike	28	M	"	"	
2655	635	McNair	Andrew	43	M	"	"	4303 "
2656	636	McNair	Jerry	34	M	Cherokee Nation	4305 "
2657	638	"	Arthur	12	M	"	"	4315 "
2658	639	"	Julia	10	F	"	"	4316 "
2659	640	"	James	8	M	"	"	4318 "

Admitted Freedmen

Miss C№	Wallace C№		Names		age	sex	Residence		
2660	641		Markham	John	26	M	Commissioners Dist №5 ? Clifton roll		
	642		See question list						
2661	643		McNair	Moses	37	M	4304	"	
2662	644 645	"		Carrie	16	F	3004	"	
2663	646	"		David	13	M	3003	"	
2664	647	"		Wm	11	M	3005	"	
2665	648	"		Johnson	8	M	3006	"	
	649		See question list						
2666	650		Meigs	George	44	M	3151	Clifton Roll	
2667	651	"		John	14	M	3152	"	
2668	652	"		Flemming	10	F	3153	"	
	653		See question list						
2669	654		Martin	Jennie	18	F	Daughter of Elias Downing 269 Admitted list		
2670	655		Meigs	Perry	26	M	Dead		
	656		See question list						
2671	657		Martin	Mary Ann	32	F			
	658 to 663		See question list						
2672	664		Murrell	Dr. Nelson	65	M	4195	Clifton roll	
2673	665		Martin	Celia	34	F	Now Bacon. See # 44210 – See 45967 for another child		
2674	666		Bacon	Maria	12	F			
2675	667		Martin	Jane	45	F	2496	Clifton roll	
2676	668	"		Clara	16	F	2500	"	
2677	669	"		Mamie	14	F	2501	"	
2678	670		Martin	Harriet	20	F	2896	"	

Admitted Freedmen

Office No.	Seller No.	Names		Age	Sex	Residence	
2679	671	Martin	Aaron	50	M	Convockamoe Dist	2892 Clifton roll
2680	672	"	George	27	M	" "	2893 "
2681	673	"	Nellie Tillie	15 14	F M	" "	Nellie 15 F wife of Chas. Thompson
2682	674	"	Josh	9	M	" "	2498 Clifton roll
2683	675	Millon	Washington	78	M	" "	3636 "
2684	676	"	Mary	40	F	" "	3637 "
2685	677	Martin	Mary	76	F	" "	
2686	678	Middleton	Tobe	23	M	" "	Son of Jennie Vann 341 Co. Dist.
	679 680	See questioned list					
2687	681	Meigs	Simon	30	M	" "	2481 Clifton roll
2688	682	"	Hattie	8	F	" "	3165 "
	683 684 685	See questioned list					
2689	686	Wurrell	Flora	53	F	" "	3062 "
2690	687	Vann	John	16	M	" "	
2691	688	Wurrell	Henry	39	M	" "	4196 "
2692	689	"	Charles	13	M	" "	4197 "
2693	690	"	John	11	M	" "	4198 "
2694	691	"	Juno	8	F	" "	4199
	692	See questioned list					
2695	693	Mayes	David	78	M	" "	
2696	694	McIntosh	Melissa	30	F	" "	1555 Clifton roll
2697	695	McLaughlin	Richd.	31	M	" "	
2698	696	Martin	Pete	44	M	Delaware Dist	2856 "

Admitted Freedmen

Office No.	Wallace No.		Names		age	Sex	Residence		
2699	697	Meigs	Peter		65	M	Cooweeskoowee Dist.	2476	Clifton roll
2700	698	"	Elizabeth		17	F	" "	2479	"
2701	699	Musgrove	Jack		63	M	" "		
2702	700	"	Walter J		16	M	" "		
2703	701	"	Eliza A		11	F	" "		
	702, 703 + 704	See questioned list							
2704	705	Morgan	John		52	M	" "	3220	"
2705	706	"	Cynthia		47	F	" "	3221	"
2706	707	Smith	Eliza		14	F	" "	}	
2707	708	"	Ollie		12	F	" "	} Wards of 705	
2708	709	"	Ella		10	F	" "	}	
	710	See questioned list							
2709	711	McNair	Lottie		29	F	" "		
2710	712	Mayfield	Robert		50	M	Illinois Dist.		
2711	713	McLain	Malinda		21	F	Sequoyah Dist.	Child of Mattie Albert No. 4 Committee list	3928 Clifton roll
2712	714	Mackey	Moses		35	M	Illinois Dist. now in Creek Nation		
2713	715	304	McClure	Dora	17	F	Sequoyah Dist	Child of Ava Yambi by McClure Dup. same as 1204.	
2714	716	McClure	Wm		24	M	" "	Brother of 715	3941 Clifton roll

Admitted Freedmen

		Names		age	Sex	Residence			
2715	717	Middleton	Lydia	40	F	Comuskonnee Dist	3998	Clifton roll
2716	718	Harper	Wm	20	M	"	"	3999	"
2717	719	"	James	18	M	"	"	4000	"
2718	720	"	Robert	16	M	"	"	4001	"
2719	721	"	Mary	13	F	"	"	4003	"
2720	722	"	Alice	13	F	"	"	4002	"
2721	723	"	Jordan	9	M	"	"	4014	
2722	724	Martin	Fred	33	M	Delaware Dist	2627	Clifton roll
2723	725	"	Jennie	34	F	"	"	3621	"
2724	726	"	Nelson	10	M	"	"	2628	"
2725	727	"	Solomon	8	M	"	"	2629	"
	728	See questioned list							
2726	729	Martin	Keaty	50	F	"	"	4154	"
2727	730	"	George	20	M	"	"	4157	"
2728	731	"	Tobe	17	M	"	"	4155	"
2729	732	"	Hanston	14	M	"	"	4158	"
2730	733	"	Sallie	12	F	"	"	4159	"
2731	734	Melton	Sawney	36	M	Comuskonna Dist		
2732	735	"	Sarah	23	F	"	"	Same as 1308	
2733	736	Melton	Amarila	38	F	"	"		
2734	737	"	Rose	17	F	"	"		
	738	See questioned list							
2735	739	Martin	Lewis	25	M	"	"	4160	Clifton roll

Admitted Freedmen

Office No.	Petition No.	Names		age	sex	Residence		
2736	740	Martin	Sarah Ann	48	F	Conneckonne Dist	2863	Clifton roll
2737	741	"	Patsey	19	F	"	" 2868	"
2738	742	"	Aaron	16	M	"	" 2864	"
2739	743	"	Joshua	12	M	"	"	
2740	744	"	Roza	10	F	"	" 2869	"
2741	745	"	Rachel	10	F	"	" 2870	"
	746	See questione list						
2742	747	Martin	Lewis	53	M	"	" 3904	"
2743	748	"	John	22	M	"	" 3905	
2744	749	"	George	20	M	"	" 3906	"
2745	750	"	Fred	15	M	"	" 3907	"
2746	751	"	Albert	8	M	"	" 3908	"
2747	752	Martin	Wm	26	M	"	"	
2748	753	Meigs	Elizabeth	60	F	"	"	See page 182 No. 40
2749	754	Markham	Harriet	65	F	"	"	
	755	See questiond list						
2750	756	Moss	Sarah E.	31	F	"	"	
2751	757	"	George H	11	M	"	"	
2752	758	"	Julia	8	F	"	"	
	759	See questione list						
2753	760	McNair	Frank	25	M	"	"	4307 Clifton roll Child of 764 Admitted list
	761	See questione list						
2754	762	Mays	Joseph	33	M	"	"	
2755	763	Mayfield	Amos	45	M	Illinois Dist		

Admitted Freedmen

Hist. No	Ledger No		Names		age	sex	Residence	
2756	764		McNair	Maria	63	F	Conuckonvee Dist	4301 Clifton roll
2757	768		Hamilton	Andrew	18	M	" "	grandchild of 764
2758	766		Mayes	David D.	31	M	" "	
2759	770	Co Dist 195	Nave	John	39	M	" "	
2760	771		Nave	George F	27	M	" "	See 340 Officlist son of Dinah Nave 354 Co Dist
2761	772		Nave	Lewis	29	M	" "	
2762	773		"	Mary	23	F	" "	
2763	774		Nave	Eli	32	M	" "	
2764	775		Nave	Wash	30	M	" "	
2765	776		Nave	Dave	35	M	" "	3837 Clifton roll See 1110, D.K. says he had a daughter born Jan 11 1883 named Heller
2766	777		Nave	Solomon	70	M	" "	
2767	778		Vivens	Santa Anna	54	M	" "	3461 Clifton roll
2768	779		Nave	Reuben	33	M	Saline Dist	3835 "
2769	780		"	Caroline	28	F	" "	4058 child of Linda French to 95 Co Dist
2770	781		"	Lulu	10	F	" "	4059 Clifton roll
2771	782		"	Lina	8	F	" "	4060 "
2772	783		Nave	Wash	65	M	" "	3836 Clifton roll
2773	785		"	George	22	M	" "	3838 "

Admitted Freedmen

Office No.	Roll No.	Names		age	Sex	Residence	
2774	786	Orr	Jesse	49	M	Tahlequah Dist	3246 Clifton roll
2775	787	O'Neil	John	25	M	Cooweescoowee Dist	
2776	788	Poleton	Riley	39	M	Illinois Dist	2728 Clifton roll
2777	789	"	Rhoda	17	F	"	"
2778	790	Prince	Annie	60	F	" "	
2779	791	"	Elmira	14	F	" "	
2780	792	Parris	Robt.	20	M	Tahlequah Dist	2801 Clifton roll
2781	793	Parris	David	19	M	" "	2803 "
2782	794	"	Sarah Ann	16	F	" "	2802 "
2783	795	Prophet	Betsey	62	F	Cooweescoowee Dist	
2784	796	Davis	Maggie	32	F	"	
2785	797	Prophet	Megira	18	F	"	
2786	798	"	Harry	16	M	" "	
2787	799	Pickett	Amelia Ann	41	F	"	
2788	800	Powell	Alexander	38	M	" "	2468 Clifton roll son of Rose Hardwick alias Chism No. 13 Delaware Dist
2789	801	Pero	Jane	38	F	Creek Nation	
2790	802	"	Eliza	14	F	" "	
2791	803	"	Benjamin	12	M	" "	Creeks and did not desire to
2792	804	"	Wm	10	M	" "	draw as Cherokees see 11291 (31)

Admitted Freedmen

Office No.	Enrollee No.	Names		age	sex	Residence	
2793	805	Parks	Celia	37	F	Conweekomee Dist.	
2794	806	Adair	Ben	24	M	" "	
2795	807	"	Josie	19	F	" "	See 2d App'y v. U. Decn 5, 4th gv 1891
2796	808	"	Abbie	16	F	" "	
2797	809	"	Peter	12	M	" "	
2798	810	"	Alexander	7	M	" "	
2799	811	Parks	Pauline	45	F	Tahlequah District	
2800	812	"	Clarence F	15	M	" "	
2801	813	"	Wm	7	M	" "	
2802	814	Pea	Susan	50	F	Delaware Dist.	3839 Clifton
2803	815	"	John	18	M	" "	3845 "
2804	816	" Laura W. or Oo-chi		13	F	" "	See 2d App'y v. U. Decn 5, 4th gv 1891 Laura Washington Pea's P. R.
2805	817	Polson	Annie		F	Greene Co. Mo.	Known also as Annie Smith. See that she is not the same as Auth. list Annie Smith. 65.F. No 1469
2806	818	Russell	Cynthia	59	F	Going Snake Dist.	
2807	819	Romeo	Rose	91	F	Illinois Dist.	
	820	823	See questioned list				
2808	824	Rogers	Samuel	24	M	Conweekomee Dist	3706 Clifton roll
2809	825	Rogers	Isaac	39	M	" "	3708 Clifton roll Husband of 813 Wal. Auth. list
2810	826	"	Cooy	8	M	" "	
2811	827	Rogers	Sarah	48	F	" "	3705 Clifton roll
2812	828	"	Wm	12	M	" "	3209 "
2813	829	"	August	11	M	" "	3210 "
2814	830	"	Henry	7	M	" "	

Admitted Freedmen

Office No	Roll No	Names		age	Sex	Residence		
2815	831	Rogers	Ellis	29	M	Connuckemme Dist	2811	Clifton roll
2816	832	Robinson	Betsey	29	F	" "	2806	Clifton roll
2817	833	Foster	Eliza	14	F	" "	2808	Clifton roll
2818	834	Martin	Jake	11	M	" "	2807	Clifton roll
2819	835	Riley	Samuel	49	M	" "	3382	"
	836	See questioned list						
2820	837	Rider	Andrew	29	M	" "	3009.	"
2821	839	Rider	George	28	M	" "	Son of Big Rider 218 Co. Dist
2822	840	Reese	Jesse	50	M	" "	2927	Clifton roll
2823	841	"	Betsey	55	F	" "	2928	"
2824	842	"	Benj	14	M	" "	2929	"
2825	843	"	Jim	12	M	" "	2930	"
2826	844	Reed	Anderson	46	M	" "		
2827	845	"	Reddy	13	M	" "		
2828	846	"	Cora	7	F	" "		
2829	847	Redbird	Maria	40	F	" "		
2830	848	"	Ugly	16	M	" "		
2831	849	"	John	13	M	" "		
2832	850	"	Susan	8	F	" "		
	851½ 854	See questioned list						
2833	855	Rogers	Josh	65	M	Tahlequah Dist		
2834	856	"	Albert	15	M	" "		

Admitted Freedmen

Office No	Index No		Names	Age	Sex	Residence	
2835	857	Roberts	Ella	35	F	Tahlequah Dist	
2836	858	"	Thomas	18	M	" "	
2837	859	"	Romey	16	M	" "	
2838	860	"	Nellie	14	F	" "	
2839	861	Riley	Joseph	83	M	" "	4075 Clifton roll
2840	862	"	Fred	15	M	" "	4079 "
2841	863	Richardson	Dora	15	F	" "	
2842	864	"	Wm	11	M	" "	
	865	see questioned list					
2843	866	Rowe	Alexis	35	M	Delaware Dist	
	867 & 869	see questioned list					
2844	870	"	Jesse	8	M		
2845	871	Ross	Joseph	49	M	Cherokee Nation	4144 Clifton roll
2846	872	"	Debby	35	F	" "	Formerly Williams
2847	873	"	Grant	16	M	" "	
2848	874	"	Phillis	14	F	" "	
2849	875	Ross	Edward St	22	M	Illinois Dist	1646 Clifton roll See # 2968 (93) Call change total, J. Ross and in 2669 & 165 filed with Wallace's approved list to 675
2850	877	Rogers	Louisa	49	F	" "	
2851	878	"	Willie	23	M	" "	
2852	879	"	Walter	19	M	" "	
2853	880	"	John	17	M	" "	
2854	881	"	Thomas	16	M	" "	
2855	882	"	Joseph	12	M	" "	
2856	883	Ross	George	26	M	Cooweescoowee Dist	4182 Clifton roll

Admitted Freedmen

Office No	Walker No	Names		ay	Sex	Residence	
2857	884	Ross	Josh	22	M	Connecknowee Dist	
2858	885	Ross	Eliza	24	F	" "	
2859	886	Rose	Emma	38	F	" "	3596 Clifton rell
2860	887	"	Eliza	20	F	" "	
2861	888	"	Charles	18	M	" "	3597
2862	889	"	Carrie	16	F	" "	3598 "
2863	890	"	Willie	13	M	" "	3599 "
2864	891	"	Mary J.	11	F	" "	3600 "
2865	892	"	Geneva	9	F	" "	3601 "
2866	893	Rogers	Isaac	53	M	" "	
2867	894	Ross	Samuel	37	M	" "	3785 "
2868	895	"	Julia	80	F	" "	
2869	896	Ross	Lewis	29	M	" "	
2870	897		Emma	28	F	" "	
2871	898	Lowe	Frank	14	M	" "	
2872	899		Wm	13	M	" "	
2873	900	Ross	Sarah E	9	F	" "	
2874	901	"	Nettie	7	F	" "	
2875	902	Rowe	George	31	M	" "	
2876	903	"	Rosella	7	F	" "	

Admitted Freedmen

Office No.	Roll No.	Names		age	Sex	Residence		
2877	904	Rowe	Delilah	36	F	Comackoma Dist		
2878	905	"	Edward	22	M	" "		
2879	907	"	Belle	16	F	" "		
2880	908	"	Fred	12	M	" "		
2881	909	"	Hattie	10	F	" "		
2882	910	"	Lonvitha	8	F	" "		
2883	911	Rowe	Joseph	54	M	" "	3455½	Clifton roll
2884	912	"	Ann	50	F	" "	3456½	"
2885	913	Ridge	Katie	74	F	Saline Dist.	3650	"
2886	914	Starr	Sallie	60	F	Sequoyah Dist.		
2887	915	Simmons	Jennie	31	F	Creek Nation	2641	Clifton roll
2888	916	Hopkins	Minnie	16	F	" "	2642	"
2889	918	Smith	Lucinda	29	F	Illinois Dist.	2617	Clifton
2890	919	"	Willie	10	M	" "	2618	"
2891	920	"	Amanda	9	F	" "	2619	"
2892	921	"	Belle	7	F	" "	2620	"
2893	922	Ross	Amanda	61	F	" "	2616	Clifton roll
2894	923	Smith	Jane	36	F	Comackoma Dist	3605 wife of Charles Smith	
2895	924	"	Eleanor	19	F	" "	3607	Clifton roll
2896	925	"	Walter	17	M	" "		
2897	926	"	Pearlie	15	F	" "	3608	"
2898	927	"	Cora	13	F	" "	3609	"
2899	928	"	Matilda	10	F	" "	3610	"
2900	929	"	Chester	8	M	" "	3611	"

Admitted Freedmen

Office No.	Wallace No.	Names		Age	Sex	Residence	
2901	930	Schaeffer	J. Wm	50	M	Convaskonva Dist.	
2902	931	"	Ollie	14	F	" "	
2903	932	"	Lillie	9	F	" "	
2904	933	"	Tillie	7	M	" "	
2905	934	Starr	Caroline	50	F	Sequoyah Dist	
2906	935	McClure	John	9	M	" "	
2907	936	Sumner	Minnie	35	F	Kansas	Child of Fred & Caroline Foreman No. 151 & 152 Illinois Dist.
2908	937	"	Rosie	4	F	"	
2909	938	"	Choteau	11	M	"	
2910	939	"	Benj	9	M	"	
2911	940	Starr	Sam	45	M	Sequoyah Dist.	
2912	941	"	Nancy	39	F	" "	2721 Clifton roll
2913	942	"	Sarah	18	F	" "	2723 "
2914	943	"	Nellie	17	F	" "	2724 "
2915	944	"	Sam H.	15	M	" "	2725 "
2916	945	"	Henry	13	M	" "	2726 "
2917	946	"	Irene	10	F	" "	
2918	947	"	Annie	8	F	" "	2727 "
2919	948	Shelton	Elias	37	M	Creek Nation	
	749	See questioned list.					
2920	950	Schrimsher	Henry	30	M	Convaskonva Dist	2579 Clifton roll
2921	951	Shad	Ida C.	18	F	Cherokee Nation	child of Joseph & Sarah Roe née Wade 2857 Clifton roll
2922	952	Shelton	Mollie	17	F	Delaware Dist	child of Pratt Martin 696 admitted list

Admitted Freedmen

Office No.	Certificate No.	Names		age	Sex	Residence				
2923	953	Shepherd	Samuel	45	M	Converskornee Dist	3810	Clifton roll		
2924	954	Smith	Moses	40	M	"	"	3419	Clifton roll	
2925	955	"	Lady Lee Eodie	15	F	"	"	3420	"	
2926	956	"	Jackson	13	M	"	"	3421	"	
2927	957	"	Thos. M.	10	M	"	"	3422	"	
2928	958	"	Sallie	8	F	"	"	3423	"	
2929	959	"	Solomon	7	M	"	"	3424	"	
2930	960 961	Smith See Question list	Joseph	36	M	"	"	3440	"	
2931	962	"	Ross	14	M	"	"	3441	"	
2932	963	"	Lena	12	F	"	"	3442	"	
2933	964	"	Isaac	10	M	"	"	3443	"	
2934	965	"	Matilda	8	F	"	"			
2935	966	Smith	Lizzie	21	F	"	"	Child of Lewis Whitmire 393 Geo. Dist		
2936	967	Smith	Caesar	22	M	"	"			
2937	968	"	Tilda	66	F	"	"	The head of the family		
2938	969	"	Susan	19	F	"	"			
2939	970	Starr	Charles	29	M	"	"	3470	Clifton roll	
2940	971	Starr See Question list	George	36	M	"	"	3642	"	
2941	972 973	"	George Jr	14	M	"	"	3643	"	
2942	974	"	Arthur	7	M	"	"	3644	"	

Admitted Freedmen

Office No.	Rolled No.	Names		age	Sex	Residence	
2943	975	Starr	Jack	52	M	Convaskonia Dist.	3469 Clifton roll
2944	976	"	Ed.	17	M	" "	3473 "
2945	977	"	Frank	15	M	" "	
2946	978	"	Elijah	14	M	" "	3476 "
2947	979	"	Delilah	12	F	" "	3475 "
2948	981	Thompson	Malinda	4	F	Illinois Dist.	Child of Pompy Sarah Thompson 434 Illinois Dist
2949	982	Taylor	Henry	26	M	Canadian Dist.	Son of Octavia Taylor, dec.d & husband 452 aunt list
2950	983	Thompson	Emma	35	F	Illinois Dist	
2951	984	"	Lewis	10	M	" "	Son of 451 Ill. Dist.
2952	965	Tyner	John	31	M	" "	4466 Clifton roll Son of Ambose Tyner 456 Ill. Dist.
	985 & 970	See question list					
2953	991	Tucker	Wm	56	M	Convaskonia Dist	4162 Clifton roll
2954	992	"	Lucinda	16	F	" "	4165 "
2955	993	"	Ella	14	F	" "	4163 "
2956	994	"	Malinda	12	F	" "	4164 "
2957	995	Tucker	Sarah P.	18	F	" "	4168 "
2958	996	Towers	John	40	M	Delaware Dist	3971 Clifton roll
2959	997	Towers	John	38	M	Saline Dist	
2960	998	Towers	Wilson	59	M	Convaskonia Dist	3503 Clifton roll
2961	999	Timmons	Horace	31	M	" "	

Admitted Freedmen

Office No.	Rollbook No.	Names		Age	Sex	Residence	
2982	1019	Thomas	Susan	15	F	Cooweeskoowee Dist.	child of Siney Thompson
2983	1020	Thomas	Rachel	21	F	" "	
2984	1021	Thomas	Harriet	15	F	" "	child of Siney Thompson
2985	1022	Tyner	Addie	26	F	Tahlequah Dist.	child of Susan Gordy 211 admitted list
2986	1023	Shepherd	Nathaniel	8	M	" "	
2987	1024	Tucker	Eliza	34	F	Delaware Dist.	child of Winnie Ratcliffe 672 Austin
2988	1025	Austin	Neal	18	M	" "	list 2819 Clifton roll
2989	1026	Taylor	James	52	M	Illinois Dist.	
2990	1027	"	Thomas	20	M	" "	
2991	1028	Taylor	John	36	M	" "	3456 Clifton roll child of Malinda or Iskey Smith 672 Ill. Dist.
2992	1029	Thompson	Polly	35	F	Muscogee Creek Nation	3247 Clifton roll
2993	1030	"	Willie	17	M	" " "	3248 "
2994	1031	Thornton	Stella	15	F	" " "	3249 "
2995	1032	"	Maud	12	F	" " "	3250 "
2996	1033	Tucker	Anna	35	F	Illinois District	wife of Lewis Tucker 432 Ill. Dist.
2997	1034	Thomas	Cynthia	25	F	Sequoyah Dist.	child of Rose Campbell

Admitted Freedmen

Off. No.	Roll No.	Names		age	Sx	Residence	4222 Clifton roll
2998	1035	Timmon	Dicie	36	F	Conuchonue Dist	child of Artie Knight & wife of 2961
2999	1036	Sorrel	Mattie	17	F	" "	and Danned dtg Sanders / 4223 Clifton roll
3000	1037	"	Morrison	15	M	" "	4224 "
3001	1038	"	Richard	13	M	" "	4225 "
3002	1039	"	Vinela	9	F	" "	4226 "
3003	1040	Todd	Wm	24	M	" "	3028 Clifton roll
	1041	See question list					
3004	1042	Thompson	Wm	13	M	Illinois Dist	Son of 2950
3005	1044	Thompson	George	68	M	Conuchonue Dist	4236 Clifton roll / Dead
3006	1045 1046 1047 1048	Thompson See question list / See after 1214	Nelson	35	M	Saline Dist	3686 Clifton roll
3007	1049	Vann	Eda	15	F	Illinois Dist / Conuchonue Dist	child of 1368
3008		"	Jennie	10	F	" "	" " "
3009	1050	Vann	Wm	61	M	Conuchonue Dist	3169 Clifton roll
3010	1051	Vann	George	49	M	" "	4041 "
3011	1052	Vann	Wm	33	M	" "	3846 "
3012	1053	Vann	Jesse	38	M	Saline Dist	3053 Clifton roll
3013	1054	"	Allen	14	M	" "	3054 "
3014	1055	"	Mollie	12	F	" "	3055 "
3015	1056	"	Walter	9	M	" "	3056 "
3016	1057	"	Frank	7	M	" "	3057 "
3017	1058	Vann	Ellis	49	M	Conuchonue Dist	2533 Clifton roll

Admitted Freedmen

No. in 30	Wallace 30		Names		age	Sex	Residence	
3018	1059	Vann		Fannie	30	F	Coovaeskmove Dist	2987 Clifton roll
3019	1060	Bean		Mary	17	F	" "	2988 "
3020	1061	Sutton		Sally	10	F	" "	2989 "
3021	1062	Vann		Jesse	27	M	" "	3841 "
3022	1063 Chap no 376	Vann		Johnson	49	M	" "	843 Clifton roll
3023	1067	"		Daisy	8	F	" "	
3024	1068	Vann		Mary	26	F	" "	Child of Mary Buffington Decd 12 Delaware Dist
	1069	See questioned list						
3025	1070	Vann		Abe	35	M	Sequoyah Dist	Brother of Jerry Vann 825 Auth. list died May 7. 1890
3026	1071	Vann		Geo. W.	75	M	" "	3937 Clifton roll
3027	1072	"		Richard	19	M	" "	
3028	1073	"		Harriem	11	M	" "	
3029	1074	O'Neil		George	7	M	" "	Son of Elmira decd daughter 8 1074
3030	1075	Vann		Jesse	19 36?	M	" "	Bro. of Jerry Vann 823 Auth. list age not given in evidence
3031	1076	Vann		Mary	15	F	Delaware Dist	
3032	1077	"		Stanford	13	M	" "	Grandchildren of Mary Buffington 570 Auth. list
3033	1078	"		Lucy	9	F	" "	
3034	1079	"		Ellis	8	M	" "	
3035	1080	Vann		Edward	18	M	" "	3570 Clifton roll Son of Wm decd Thos Mayfield guar
3036	1081	Vann		Charlotte	70	F	Coovaeskove Dist	
3037	1082	Smith		James (imbecile)	30	M	" "	Son of 1081 (an imbecile)

Admitted Freedmen

Official No.	Dawes No.	Names		age	sex	Residence	
3038	1083	Vann	Joshua	30	M	Cooweescoowee Dist	3840 Clifton roll
3039	1085	Venton	Joseph	37	M	" "	4210 "
3040	1086	Vann	Susan	55	F	Illinois Dist	
3041	1087	Vann	Ebbie	53 17	F	" "	child of 1932 Affirm. See his affid. Bennett say should not be at his age less no 54. Bennett is wrong. See letter to him Oct 27, 1891 224 of change age isch
3042	1088	Vann	Isaac	25	M	" "	
3043	1090	Vann	Andrew J	18	M	Tahlequah Dist	Children of Winter Vann 683 aunt list No 52 Del. Dist.
3044	1091	"	George	15	M	" "	
3045	1093	Walker	Frances	19	F	" "	
3046	1094	Whitmire	Ezekiel	16	M	Cooweescoowee Dist	child of Dick Whitmire 412 Coo Dist
3047	1095	Putnam	Katie	11	F	" "	Grand child " " "
3048	1099	Wolf	Charles	18	M	411H Clifton "	Louis Nave No 190 aunt
3049	1100	"	Solomon	16	M	4112 Clifton "	list their guardian
3050	1102	Wilson	Oliver	36	M	Tahlequah Dist	3253 Clifton roll
3051	1103	Wilson	Jacob B.	32	M	" "	3254 "
3052	1104	Wright	Ruth	34	F	Illinois Dist	
3053	1105	"	Cora	17	F	" "	
3054	1106	"	Henry	15	M	" "	
3055	1107	"	Cornelius	13	M	" "	

Admitted Freedmen

Office No	Landless No	Names		age	sex	Residence			
3056	1108	Wolf	Susie	60	F	Illinois Dist			
3057	1109	"	Nancy	15	F	"	"		
3058	1110	"	Mary	10	F	"	"		
3059	1111	Whitmire	Jesse	33	M	Cowaskowwa Dist		3784	Clifton roll
3060	1113	"	Sim	17	M	"	"	3541	Clifton roll
3061	1113	"	Samuel	15	M	"	"	3547	"
3062	1114	"	Guela	8	F	"	"		
3063	1115	West	Henry	83	M	Sequoyah Dist			
3064	1116	"	George	22	M	"	"	2719	Clifton roll
3065	1117	West	Lizzie	25	F	"	"	Wife of Houston West 1118 admitted
3066	1118	West	Houston	34	M	"	"	2718	Clifton roll
3067	1119	"	John	12	M	"	"		
3068	1120	"	Callis	10	M	"	"	2730	"
3069	1121	"	Ida	8	F	"	"	2731	"
3070	1122	West	Callis	36	M	"	"	2717	Clifton roll
3071	1123	"	Ada	12	F	"	"	2740	"
3072	1124	"	Maria	9	F	"	"	2741	"
3073	1125	"	Henry	7	M	"	"	2742	"
3074	1126	Whitmire	Mary	24	F	"	"		
3075	1127	Williams	Eleanor	32	F	"	"	3538	"
3076	1128	"	Jimmie	11	M	"	"	3539	"

Admitted Freedmen

Office No	Dawes No		Names		age	sex	Residence	
3077	1129		Wright	Mary	24	F	Sequoyah Dist.	3942 Clifton roll Daughter of Geo. Y. born 1071 admd. L.4
3078	1130		Hill	Cornelia	11	F	" "	3943 Clifton roll
3079	1131		"	Anna	8	F	" "	3944 Clifton roll
3080	1132		"	Pearlie	7	F	" "	3945 Clifton roll
3081	1133		West	Hannah	65	F	" "	
3082	1134		Holt	Louisa J.	21	F	" "	grand-daughter of 1133
3083	1135		Wright	Savilla	45	F	Cooweeskoowee Dist	3582 Clifton roll Child of Lucinda Wright 453 born. Dist
3084	1136	109	"	George	12	M	813 Clifton roll	Duplicate see 813 du 14 291 (91) grandchild of 1135. Sustd he is not the same George might as 109 - Sequoyah Dist.
3085	1138		Whitmire	James	38	M	Delaware Dist	
3086	1139		Webber	Andy	35	M	Saline Dist	
3087	1140		"	Wm	10	M	" "	
3088	1143		Wright	Ruth	32	F	Cooweeskoowee Dist	Child of Snonda Wright 411 auch. Dist
3089	1144		"	Thomas	9	M	" "	
3090	1145		"	Stephen	7	M	" "	
3091	1146		Wright	Edward	36	M	" "	2997 Clifton roll
3092	1147		"	John H.	15	M	" "	2998 "
3093	1148		"	David M.	12	M	" "	See No 411 N 5567

Admitted Freedmen

Office No	Folio No		Names	age	Sex	Residence			
3094	1149	Wilson	Amelia	37	F	Crockerville Dist			
3095	1150	"	Florence	19	F	"	"		
3096	1151	"	Mamie	17	F	"	"		
3097	1152	"	John	15	M	"	"		
3098	1153	"	George	14	M	"	"		
3099	1154	"	Edward	12	M	"	"		
3100	1155	"	Frances	10	F	"	"		
3101	1156	"	Allie	7	F	"	"		
3102	1157	Williams	Lizzie	37	F	"	"	4213 Clifton roll	
3103	1158	454	Williams	Amanda	48	F	"	"	
3104	1162	Whitmire	Daniel	31	M	"	"	2494 Clifton roll	
3105	1163	Whitmire	Hester	43	F	"	"		
3106	1164	Candy	Jim	15	M	"	"		
3107	1165	"	Lizzie	14	F	"	"		
3108	1166	Whitmire	Mike	63	M	"	"		
3109	1167	Whitmire	Samuel	35	M	"	"	3400	"
3110	1169	Whitmire	Frank	40	M	"	"	3710	"
3111	1170	"	Rachel	19	F	"	"	3711	"
3112	1171	"	Eliza	17	F	"	"	3712	"
3113	1172	"	Oscar	15	M	"	"	3713	"
3114	1173	"	Anna	13	F	"	"	3714	"
3115	1174	"	Helen	12	M	"	"	3716	"
3116	1175	"	Ellen	7	F	"	"	3715	"

Admitted Freedmen

Hire No	Welfare No	Names		age	sex	Residence	
3117	1176	Webber	Becky	82	F	Connectima Dist	3497 Clifton rd
3118	1177	Webber	Aaron	35	M	"	"
3119	1178	Webber	Robert	45	M	"	"
3120	1180	"	Frank	19	M	"	"
3121	1181	"	Josh	17	M	"	"
3122	1182	"	Samuel	15	M	"	"
3123	1183	"	Ellen	13	F	"	"
3124	1184	Webber	Harriet	31	F	"	"	wife of 1194 3157 Clifton
3125	1185	"	Moses	13	M	"	"
3126	1186	"	Wesley	11	M	"	"
3127	1187	"	Edward H	9	M	"	"
3128	1188	Webb	Jane	35	F	"	"	4004 Clifton roll
3129	1189	Brown	Eddie	18	M	"	"	4005 "
3130	1190	Webber	Nelson	64	M	"	"
3131	1191	Webber	Wm	39	M	"	"	4074 " child of Linda French 9560 Dis
3132	1192	"	Charles	8	M	"	"
3133	1193	"	Ida May	7	F	"	"	Born after Mar 3.1883 14291 (9) " Dec.16.1883 14715
3134	1194	Webber	Ellis	40	M	"	"	3457 Clifton roll husband of 1184
3135	1195	Water	Sandy S	33	M	"	"	Dup of 2977 see 14291 (9) Tax pay roll
3136	1197	"	Alpha	8	F	"	"

Admitted Freedmen

Hiss No	Sellow No		Names		age	sex	Residence			
3137	1198	Watie	Andrew T		35	M	Conceskena Dist	3561	Clifton roll
3138	1199	"	Mary		25	F	"	"	3562	"
3139	1200	"	Fred T		13	M	"	"		
3140	1201	"	Rufus T		11	M	"	"	3563	"
3141	1202	"	Maggie T		9	F	"	"	3564	"
3142	1203	Warren	Matilda		55	F	"	"	3786	"
3143	1204	Johnson	John		27	M	"	"	3787	"
3144	1206	Warren	Willis		14	M	"	"	Child of Ellis Warren
3145	1207	"	Carrie		12	F	"	"	" " " "
3146	1208	"	Callis		10	M	"	"	" " " "
3147	1209	Ward	Berry		41	M	"	"	
3148	1210	"	George		17	M	"	"	
3149	1211	Ward	Squire		37	M	"	"	3080 Clifton roll
3150	1213	"	Sadie		12	F	"	"	3084 "
3151	1214	"	Joseph		7	M	"	"	3085 "
3152	1048	Vann	Halie		17	F	"	"	4191 Error. Child of Eli Vann 23 Co. Dist
3153	1217	Ward	Ben		32	M	"	"	3079 Clifton roll
3154	1218	"	Lena		8	F	"	"	3101 Clifton roll
3155	1219	Ward	Alexander		37	M	"	"	3812 Error
3156	1220	"	Hayes		10	M	"	"	"
3157	1221	"	Henrietta		8	F	"	"	3107 "
3158	1222	"	Irving		7	M	"	"	3108 "

Admitted Freedmen

Off. No.	Dollar No.	Names		age	sex	Residence	
3159	1223	Webber	Andy	13	M	Conucchecmee Dist	
3160	1224	"	Carrie	11	F	" "	Children of Johnson Webber Dec.d
3161	1225	"	Annie	9	F	" "	Jno O'Neil No 787 admr
3162	1226	Ward	Abraham	44	M	" "	30 78 Clifton roll
3163	1228	"	Alonzo	23	M	" "	3088 "
3164	1229	"	Ibon	21	M	" "	3089 "
3165	1230	"	Eliza	19	F	" "	3090 "
3166	1231	"	Sarah	18	F	" "	"
3167	1232	"	Berry	16	M	" "	3091 "
3168	1233	"	Daniel	10	M	" "	3092 "
3169	1234	"	Lina	9	F	" "	3093 "
3170	1235	Ward	Peter	65	M	" "	3077 Clifton roll
3171	1237	"	David	30	M	" "	3083 "
3172	1238	"	Clinton	29	M	" "	
3173	1239	"	Martha	25	F	" "	
3174	1240	Rowe	Grant	16	M	" "	
3175	1241	"	Sherman	14	M	" "	
3176	1242	"	Lewis	12	M	" "	Grand children of Peter Ward 1235
3177	1243	"	Phebe	10	F	" "	
3178	1244	Woodall	Ches	39	M	Sequoyah Dist	
3179	1245	Young	Nellie	29	F	Conucheemee Dist	
3180	1246	Johnson	Harrison	35	M	Cherokee Nation	3399 Clifton roll
3181	1247	"	Harry	11	M	" "	
3182	1248	"	Callie	7	F	" "	

Admitted Freedmen

Office No.	Claimant No. (Register List)	Names		age	Sex	Residence	
3183	162	Bruner	Joseph	53	M	Sequoyah Dist	C. B. Bright Master
3184	495	Hayden	Maria	69	F	Conoeskinne Dist	254 Clifton Geo. Whitmire Master
3185	884	Ridge	Cornelius	39	M	Saline Dist	3851 Clifton Herman Ridge Master
3186	885	"	Allena	18	F	" "	
3187	886	"	Ida B	15	F	" "	
3188	887	"	Henry C.	13	M	" "	3864 Clifton
3189	888	"	Amanda G.	11	F	" "	3865 "
3190	889	"	Laura M	9	F	" "	
3191	1130	Vann	James	31	M	Conoeskinne Dist	2597 Clifton Col. Vann Master
3192	1131	"	Sam	17	M	" "	2598 "
3193	1132	"	Rufus	15	M	" "	2599 "
3194	1133	"	Martha	12	F	" "	2600 "
3195	1134	"	Wm	9	M	" "	2601 "

Free Negroes

Office No.	Roll No. Admitted list	Names		age	44	Residence	
3196	375	Gibson	Poe	66	M	Convaskrvva Dist	
	Truslist						
3197	1	Manley	Alonza	39	M	" "	3732 Clifton roll
3198	2	"	Almira	11	F	" "	on apptint doched of Cherokee Iolwerars
3199	3	"	Amanda	8	F	" "	as Nos. 387-388 hit out of schedule add.
3200	7	Mayfield	Thomas	66	M	Saline Dist	2880 Clifton roll
3201	8	"	Nancy y Thiey	56	F	" "	
3202	9	"	Charles	35	M	" "	2861 "
3203	10	Rankin	Uren	40	M	Illinois Dist	2671 Clifton roll
3204	11	"	Thomas	16	M	" "	2672 "
3205	12	"	Matthew	14	M	" "	2673 "
3206	13	"	Birdie	11	F	" "	2674 "
3207	14	Roberson	Jobe R.	27	M	Convaskrvva Dist	2982 "
3208	15	Roberson	Wesley	25	M	" "	
3209	16	Roberson	Wm H.	38	M	" "	2972 "
3210	17	"	Josie Ann	15	F	" "	2973 "
3211	18	"	Miey J.	11	F	" "	2974 "
3212	19	"	Eva E	9	F	" "	2975 "
3213	20	"	James	7	M	" "	2976 "
3214	24	Vann	Maggie	23	F	Illinois Dist	Daughter of No 10 this schedule
3215	25	Hampton	Adeline	35	F	" "	
3216	26	Dash	Nora	18	F	" "	

Department of the Interior
Office Indian Affairs
October 29th 1890

The foregoing schedule, containing the names of 1988 living and 107 dead freedmen, who are, or have been, recognized as such by the Cherokee Authorities, or are the children of such; of 1087 who were "admitted" by Special Agent Wallace as entitled to have, (with the Shawnees and the Delawares) in the per capita distribution of the sum of seventy five thousand dollars ($75.000) appropriated by the Act of October 19. 1888, (25 Stats, p. 609) and whose decision is sustained by the evidence presented; of 13 who were rejected by Special Agent Wallace, as not entitled &c, but the evidence presented in each case shows that they were the slaves, or the children of slaves, of Cherokee Indians, who returned to the Nation within the limit of time fixed by the 9th Article of the treaty of July 19. 1866 (14 Stats, p. 801) and who continued to reside and still reside within the limits of said Nation; and of 21 persons known as "free colored persons who were in the country at the commencement of the rebellion and are now resident therein," and their descendants, making in the aggregate 3216 persons who, in my judgement, are entitled, from the evidence and facts presented in Special Agent Wallace's report, to share in the per capita distribution of the sum of seventy five thousand dollars appropriated as aforesaid and as in the said Act provided; and I respectfully submit the same, with the recommendation that it be approved by you and that a per capita payment of fifteen dollars and fifty cents ($15.50) be made to each of said claimants; that being the sum to which each is entitled to receive under the law.

R. V. Belt
Acting Commissioner

Department of the Interior
Nov. 21st 1890
The foregoing Schedule of 3216 names from
page 1 to page 154 is hereby approved as recommended.
John W. Noble
Secretary

Copy sent to Agent Bennett Dec 9 - 1890   208/
                                            456

157

Questioned List

	Wallace No. / Bell	Names		Age	Sex	Residence	
1	1	Alberty	George	26	M	Tahlequah Dist	No evidence that he or his parents were slaves of Cherokees.
2	19	"	Alice	13	F	Cooweescoowee Dist	Vouched for as the child of Guessett Jane Alberty, but no evidence to identify parents as slaves of Cherokees
3	58	Bell	George C	23	M	Sequoyah Dist	No evidence to show that these parties are the children of 2147 or 2148.
4	59	"	Emily	16	F	" "	
5	60	"	Nancy Ann	14	F	" "	
6	61	"	Arthur	9	M	" "	
7	74	Buffington	Mattie	24	F	Tahlequah Dist	Nativity of parents lacking or that they were slaves of Cherokees.
8	89	Bolyn	Elizabeth	26	F	Cooweescoowee Dist	No evidence that they are the children of Cher. freedmen 2537 Clifton valle and ore. evid. that 91 was Born aug. 1883 & evid. in 91 born before Mar. 3.1883.
9	90	"	Amelia	9	F	" "	
10	91	"	Henrietta	6	F	" "	
11	133	Bean	Clarinda No name given	36	F	" "	John Bean No 2215 says she is his wife & a citizen of the Nation slave of Lucy Martin Does he mean that she was not a slave of a Cherokee?
12	161	Blackburn	Ellen	30	F	" "	Parents not given. No evidence that she was slave of a Cherokee
13	183	Cross	Jennie	23	F	Tahlequah Dist	No evidence as to parents or that they were slaves of Cherokees
14	193	Choate	Sherman	7	M	Illinois Dist	Is not this a duplicate of 1026 The same says B 14704 (91)
15	212	Colbert	Hattie	23	F	Cooweescoowee Dist	Lacks evidence as to parents whether or not they are slaves of Cherokees

Questioned List

	Roll No.	Names		age	sex	Residence	
16	219	Cherry	Betty	18	F	Connecticoma Dist.	No evidence that parents were slaves of Cherokee Indian.
17	222	Cordy	Kate	46	F	" "	⎫ Lewis Cordy, the husband, offers
18	223	Roach	Jesse	28	M	" "	⎪ no evidence that his wife was the
19	224	Chambers	Harry	21	M	" "	⎬ slave of a Cherokee, & so the
20	225	Thompson	Lucinda	18	F	" "	⎪ children are here & without their status
21	226	"	Daniel	1½6	M	" "	⎪ dependent on her being such a slave
22	227	Ross	Thomas	7	M	" "	⎭
23	243	Daniels	Frank	28	M	Cherokee Nation	⎫ No evidence that he was the
24	244	"	Wm	7	M	" "	⎬ slave of a Cherokee Indian.
25	303	Calon	Nettie	22	F	Saline Dist	No evidence as to her parents or that they were Cherokee slaves
26	315	Fields	Wm H.	30	M	Tahlequah Dist.	Wm H. claims to be the
27	316	"	Elias	9	M	" "	son of Abraham & Sally Field Nos. 1051 & 1052, he also claims that his father was 52 years old when he died, whereas Abraham No. 1051 was living.
28	317	French	Susan	38	F	Connecticoma Dist.	The evidence submitted
29	318	"	Amanda	17	F	" "	defective in that it is signed by Peter Melton, whilst it purports to have been given by George Melton and does not furnish proof that either his wife said Susan or her child, was the slave or child of slave of a Cherokee Indian

	Roll No.	Names		age	sex	Residence	
30	320	Foster _{née Walker} Sarah		23	F	Cooweescoowee Dist.	No evidence that she is the child of a Cherokee slave.
31	323	French _{née Markham} Charlotte		30	F	" "	No evidence that she was the slave of a Cherokee Indian.
32	343	Ford	Rhoda	19	F	Tahlequah Dist.	No evidence that she is the child of a Cherokee slave.
33	360	Grimmett _{née Vizer} Peggy		22	F	Cooweescoowee Dist.	Wife of Henderson Grimmett No 119, but no evidence that she was the child of a Cherokee slave.
34	364	Gunter	Phillis	45	F	" "	Wife of Henry Gunter No 2410 but no evidence that she was the slave of a Cherokee Indian.
35	365	Groomer	Della	19	F	Kansas, Thayer	The child of Jonah Ragsdale, No 272, but as she has always lived in Kansas and was not given in by her father in his enrollment of his family, it is necessary that further proof shall be furnished from her, or her father, as to her mother, or why she was not referred to in his enrollment.
36	436	Hicks	Lydia	16	F	Tahlequah Dist.	Formerly Ridge, claims that her parents were slaves, but taken off in 1859 in Mo. & came back in 1866 to the Nation. Must furnish proof that parents were returned by to Cherokees Feb. 1863 when the Nation abolished slavery or be rejected as a claimant

Questioned List

	Freedmen No?	Names		age	sex	Residence	
37	468	Johnson see p 192	David	25	M	Delaware Dist.	No evidence that he was the child of a Cherokee slave.
38	489	Hill	Katie	53	F	Creek Nation	Claims to be the child of Lucy Rider, to 276, who was but 60 years old. Reconcile ages.
39	500	King	Mollie	24	F	Illinois Dist.	Claims to be the grand daughter of Jesse Edmunds to 175 on Cherokee roll, Illinois Dist who was only 41 years old when he died in 1881.
40	507	Leak	Elizabeth	25	F	Cooweeskoowee Dist	No evidence that she was the child of a Cherokee slave.
41	515	Looney	Josie	30	F	" "	No evidence that she was the slave of a Cherokee
42	518	Lyons	Ned	19	M	Cherokee Nation	Who born & raised in Cher.
43	579	"	Rachel	17	F	" "	Nation no evidence that they
43½		Lyons	Winnie	20	F	wife of George Lyons	are the children of Cherokee freedmen.
44	520	Lyons	Elias	23	M	Delaware Dist.	No evidence that he was the child of a Cher. freedman
45	579	Martin	Mike	24	M	Cooweeskoowee Dist	No evidence that he was the child of a Cherokee freedman
46	581	Martin	Mary C.	18	F	Delaware Dist.	Jobe Martin, claims that she is his wife, and aged 18 years & that Nathan Martin step-son & 14,704 as claimer the age aged 14 or 18 yrs is their son. There is no evidence showing that she is the slave a the child a a slave of a Cherokee Indian.

	Roll No.	Names		age	sex	Residence	
47	588	Maye	Cynthia	14	F	Cooweescoowee Dist	Her guardian Philip Fotube 91 says she is the child of George Maye dec'd but there is no evidence furnished that he was a Cherokee freedman, his name not being on the Auth. list furnished by the Cherokee Authorities
48	595	Mackey	Rufus	20	M	Illinois Dist	Said to be the son of Judith Freeman, now keeps etc. was but no evidence or papers to be found being lost or mislaid
49	619	McNair	Ruth	23	F	Cooweescoowee Dist	No evidence that she was the child of the slave of a Cher. Indian
50	637	McNair	Hannah	28	F	Cherokee Nation	No evidence that she was the slave of a Cherokee Indian
51	642	Markham	Charlotte	19	F	Cooweescoowee Dist	No evidence that she was the child of a slave of a Cher. Indian
52 52½	644	McNair McIntosh	Jennie Betty	48 23	F F	" "	No evidence that she was the slave of a Cherokee Indian
53	649	McNair	Elmore	6	M F	" "	There should be evidence furnished that she was born before March 3 1863. Some on file. Born Jan 4, 1861 see 1843-9
54	653	Martin	John	24	M	" "	No evidence that he was the slave of a Cherokee freedman
55	656	Meigs	Florence	28 24	F	" "	No evidence that she was the child of a Cher. freedman

	No.	Names		age	sex	Residence	
56	658	Mayfield	Charles	36	M	Cooweescoowee Dist	Charles states that he was a slave
57	659	"	Maggie	35	F	" "	& recognized voter, but no evidence
58	660	Thompson	Cornelius	15	M	" "	that he or his wife were slaves of
59	661	Mayfield	Emma	12	F	" "	Cher. Indians. Her child Cornelius
60	662	"	Malinda	9	F	" "	& the 3 children contingent upon
61	663	"	Nancy	8	F	" "	establishing the status of parents
62	679	Martin	Israel	24	M	" "	No evidence that they were
63	680	"	Lizzie	22	F	" "	children of Cherokee freedmen
64	683	Martin	Mary Ann	26	F	" "	No evidence that Mrs. Martin
65	684	Peterson	Lavina	12	F	" "	was the slave, or the child of a
66	685	"	Charity	9	F	" "	slave of Cherokee Indians.
							Her status fixes that of the
							two children.
67	692	Mayes	Harry	23	M	" "	No evidence that he was
							the son of Cherokee freedman
68	702	Musgrove	Clarinda	6	F	" "	Evidence must be furnish-
							ed that she was born prior to
							Mar 3. 1883.
69	703	Musgrove	Wm	24	M	" "	The affidavit in this case is
							signed by Musgrove. Is the
							name of claimant Willie, Wm
							or Henry? Establish the fact
							by further evidence that he is
							the son of a Cherokee freedman
							The affidavit only claims
							his father as such. Let the
							fact, if true be fully
							established.

Questioned List

	Roll No.	Names		ag	sex	Residence	
70	704	Moore	Wm	25	M	Delaware Dist	No evidence that he was the son of a Cherokee freedman
71	710	Morgan	Mary	24	F	Saline Dist	Born in Kansas, no evidence as to who were her parents or that they were Cherokee freedmen
72	728	Martin	Sylvester	6	M	Delaware Dist	Endorsed Aug 3 2141 Evidence must be furnished that he was born prior to Mar 3, 1883
73	738	Martin	Samuel	24	M	Cooweescoowee Dist	Born since Mar 3, 1883 See Sept 4, 1904 (q) No evidence as to who were his parents, or that they were Cherokee freedmen.
74	746	Martin	Ose	6	M	" "	Evidence must be furnished that he was born before Mar. 3, 1883. Born after Mar 3 1883; Sept 4 1904. (q1)
75	755	Rogers	Cloe	15	F	" "	Harriet Markham No 2749, with whom she lives, says she is the child of a Cherokee by blood others aver that she is the child of Dido Chouteau, who died in '76, the slave of Jim Chouteau. Let the fact be ascertained whether or no he received pay out of the $300,000 as the child of a Cherokee by blood
76	759	Moss	John S	6	M	" "	Evidence must be furnished that he was born prior to Mar. 3, 1883. Born after Mar 3 1883; Sept 4 1904
77	761	McNair	Mary	26	F	" "	Wife of Frank, but no evidence that she was the child of a Cherokee freedman
78	767	Munson	Minnie	18	F	See 2033 Tejas roll	No evidence that parents were Cherokee freedmen

Questioned List

	Roll No	Names		age	Sex	Residence	
79	768	Nave	Mattie	20	F	Cooweescoowee Dist	Said to be the child of Sol. Nave No. 2766, but no evidence or papers furnished in her case. If furnished lost or mislaid
80	769	Nash	John	23	M	" "	No evidence that parents were Cherokee freedmen.
81	784	Nave	Maria	65	F	Saline Dist	No evidence that she was the slave of a Cherokee Indian
82	820	Rogers	Aggie	32	F	" "	Wife of Jim Rogers No 895
83	821	Nave	Susan	11	F	" "	but no evidence that she or her
84	822	"	Amanda	8	F	" "	children were the children of Cherokee freedmen.
85	823	Rogers	Mary	22	F	Cooweescoowee Dist	No evidence as to who were her parents or that they were Cherokee freedmen
86	836	Ridge	Eleann	8	F	" "	Case of 2811 Grand-daughter of Katie Ridge No 2885, but no evidence that her parents were slaves of Cherokee Indians
87	851	Rector	Wm	26	M	" "	No evidence that they were the children of Cher. freedmen
88	852	" née Thompson	Anna	21	F	" "	
89	853	Ratcliffe née Johnson	Eda	27	F	" "	Require evidence that she is not the Eda Ratcliffe of Delaware Dist, No 658. This party claims to have been the slave of David Carter, wife of Isaac Ratcliffe

	Wallace No	Names		age	sex	Residence	
90	854	Ratcliffe	Eliza	70	F	Cooweescoowee Dist	Require evidence that she is not the Eliza Ratcliffe (Tahlequah Dist, No 784. This party claims to have been the slave of Wm Ratcliffe
91	865	Lynch	Myrtie	8	F	Tahlequah Dist	The claim in this case is made by the grand-mother, Virginia Ratcliffe, No 660, who states that her daughter was enrolled in Delaware Dist. Require evidence that she is not the Myrtie Lynch (Del Dist No 617 Confd List of No 617 see 14,704
92	867	Rowe	Rose	38	F	Delaware Dist	Require evidence that these parties are different from the Rose, Perry & Celia Rowes
93	868	"	Perry	15	M	" "	
94	869	"	Celia	13	F	" "	1984 to 1986. They are claimed by Alexis Rowe No 2843 as his wife and children Confd List of No 1984 & 1986 Sup 784
95	949	Scott	Omie	19	F	Creek Nation	Claims to be the child of one Jesse Ridge, who the state was also an applicant. No evidence that parents were Cherokee freedmen.
96	961	Smith	Eliza	36?	F	Cooweescoowee Dist	No evidence as to age or that she was the slave of a Clark
97	972	Starr	Malinda	33	F	" "	" No evidence that she was the slave of a Cherokee Indian

Questioned List

	Vol. No	Names		age	sex	Residence	
98	986	Tuckey	Jeff	61	M	Delaware Dist.	The evidence shows that the
99	987	"	Cornelius	33	M	" "	three first named were slaves who
100	988	"	Eli	27	M	" "	were removed to Texas before the
101	989	"	Martin	11	M	" "	war, but no evidence when they re-
102	990	"	Wa-ha-chi	7	M	" "	turn? Require evidence when they
							returned, & that they have main-
							tained a continuous residence in
							Cher. Nation ever since return.
103	1041	Todd	Rachel	15	F	Coweehowee Dist.	No evidence as to who were her
							parents or that they were Cherokee
							freedmen. Daughter of 2645.
104	1046	Vann	Isaac	15	M	" "	Children of George Vann and
105	1047	Whitmire	Jacob	10	M	" "	Martin Whitmire and
			Albert	6	M		grand children of Fred Markham
						Born Jany 1863	No 178. As the parents could not be
							found on the Authentic'd rolls
							furnished by Cher. Auth. evidence
							must be furnished showing that
							said parents were Cherokee freedmen
106	1069	Vann	Charles	24	M	" "	No evidence as to who were his
							parents or that they were Cherokee
							freedmen. Son of 2689.
107	1084	Vann	Eliza	24	F	" "	No evidence as to who were her
							parents or that they were —
							Cherokee freedmen. Sister of Hero
108	1089	Vann	Benjamin	25	M	Tahlequah Dist.	No evidence as to who were
							his parents or that they were
							Cherokee freedmen.
							Son of 3040

		Names		age	Sex	Residence	
109	1096	Whitmire	Patsey	19	F	Cooweeskoowa Dist	Wife of Nathan Whitmire No. 438, but no evidence as to who her parents were, or that they were Cherkee Freedmen. Jan 11 Aug 2811
110	1097	Whitmire	Lucinda	17	F	" "	Wife of Legal Whitmire No 489, but no evidence as to who are her parents or that they were Cherokee freedmen
111	1098	Ward	George	23	M	" "	Husband of Nancy Ward No. 441, but no evidence that his parents were Cherkee freedmen. Ser. of 3170
112	1101	Wilson	Susie	12	F	" "	No evidence submitted or found with this case.
113	1137	Whitmire	Jane	25	F	" "	Wife of Dick Whitmire No 445, but no evidence that parents were Cherokee Freedmen.
114	1141	Wolf	Grant	22	M	" "	Grant Wolf states that his parents and those of his wife were slaves, but fails to give their names or their owners names, or that they were slaves of Cher. Indian
115	1142	"	Pliny	21	F	" "	
116	1159	Whitmire	Elizabeth	20	F	" "	Wife of Johnson Whitmire dec'd No 2072, but no evidence furnished that she was the child of a Cher. freedman. Requires evidence that she is not the party registered as 2463 Dup. of 2463. See 14764. (91)

Questioned List

	Rolls No.	Names		age	sex	Residence	
117	1160	Whitmire	Mike	26	M	Cooweescoowee Dist	No evidence as to who were his parents, or that they were Cherokee Freedmen
118	1161	Whitmire	Kate	29	F	" "	Wife of Noben Whitmire dec'd No. 2074, but no evidence as to who were her parents, or whether she or they were the slaves of Cherokee freedmen. Daughters of 2155 & 2156.
119	1168	Whitmire nee Wilber	Lydia	30	F	" "	Wife of Sam Whitmire No. 3109, but no evidence as to lineage or whether she, or her parents, were the slaves of Cherokee Indians Daughter of 3117
120	1179	Nebbes Stille, Eliza Manly Kate	Margaret	55 39 23	F F F	" "	Wife of Robert Nebbes No. 3119, but no evidence that she was the slave of a Cherokee Indian.
121	1196	Watie	Ophelia J.	27	F	" "	Wife of Sandy J Watie No 3135, but no evidence as to who are her parents or that she or they are Cherokee freedmen
122	1205	Warren Not a claimant, See 14704	Ellis	42	M	" "	No evidence furnished that he was the slave of a Cherokee Indian or that he was ever a claimant

Questioned List

	Roll No.	Names		age	sex	Residence	
123	1212	Ward nee Mayes Mary			F	Coonaskoowe Dist	Wife of Squire Ward No 3149, but no evidence that she or her parents were Cherokee freedmen. Daughter of 2695
124	1215	Ward	Emanuel	20	M	" "	No evidence furnished that he is the child of a slave of a Cherokee Indian Son of 2343
125	1216	Ward	Maria	24	F	" "	No evidence furnished that she is the child of a Cher. Indian Daughter of 2461
126		Ward	Amanda	28	F	" "	Wife of Alexander Ward, No. 3155, Name omitted by Special Agent Wallace and no evidence furnished that she or her parents were Cherokee freedmen.
127	1227	Ward	Caroline	49/44	F	" "	Wife of Abraham Ward No 3162, but no evidence furnished as to her age, or that she or her parents were slaves of Cherokee Indian.
128	1236	Ward	Louisa	64	F	" "	Wife of Peter Ward No 3170, but no evidence furnished that she was the slave of a Cherokee Indian.

Questioned List

	Roll No.	Names		ap	Sex	Residence	
129	1249	Landrum	Charles	22	M	Cooweescoowee Dist.	No evidence furnished that parents were the slaves of Cherokee Indians.
		See evidence in #643 - 9. Same as 2596. See #14704					
130		Vann	Emma	35	F	Saline District	Wife of Jesse Vann, No. 3012, and said to have been the slave of Dr. Thornton Daughter of 2756, Sister of 2639, 3709, 2655 & 2661.

Dep

Department of the Interior
Office Indian Affairs
October 29th 1890

The foregoing "questioned list" contains the names of 130 persons claiming to be freedmen under the 9th Article of the Cherokee treaty of July 19. 1866 (14 Stat. p. 801) and "admitted" by Special Agent — John W. Wallace as entitled to share with the Freedmen, Shawnees & Delawares in the per capita distribution of the sum of $75.000. appropriated by the Act of October 19. 1888 (25 Stat. p. 609), but in my judgement, are not sufficiently supported by the evidence presented by him to justify enrollment as claimants entitled to share in the distribution of said sum of $75.000   I therefore respectfully recommend that a copy of the list, with the evidence furnished, be forwarded to Leo E. Bennett, U.S. Indian Agent at Muscogee, Indian Territory, with instructions that the parties named therein be notified that they will be required to supply the lacking evidence specified in each case before their names will be submitted for your decision whether or not, they or any of them shall be added to the schedule of those who are entitled to share in the per capita distribution of the aforesaid sum of $75.000 & that he, the agent, be required to make early report thereon to this office.

R. V. Belt,
Acting Commissioner.

Department of the Interior
Apr. 21. 1890

I concur in the foregoing, and direct that the necessary instructions be issued

John W. Noble
Secretary

Supplemental Schedule of names of "Cherokee —
Freedmen" made by John W Wallace, U. S. Special Agent,
and reported to the Department October 29. 1890 as a
"Questioned List" (See pages 157—171) and recommended for
final enrollment by U. S. Indian Agent Leo E. Bennett,
under his instruction of December 19. 1890, as entitled to
share with the Delawares and Shawnees in the per capita
distribution of the sum of $75.000 appropriated by the
Act of Congress, approved October 19. 1888 (25 Stats, p. 609) &
revised under the supervision of this Office.

O.R. No.	V.R. No.	List No.	Names		age	sex	Residence			
3217	19	2	Alberty	Alice	15	F	Cooweeskoowee Dist			
3218	89	8	Bowlyn or Bowlin	Elizabeth	27	F	"	"	2535 Clifton roll
3219	90	9	" "	Aurelia	10	F	"	"	2536	"
3220	133	11	Bean	Clarinda	37	F	"	"	3660	"
3221	161	12	Blackburn	Ellen	30	F	"	"	2531 Clifton roll
3222	183	13	Cross	Jennie	25	F	Tahlequah Dist			
3223	212	15	Colbert	Hattie	24	F	Cooweeskoowee Dist			
3224	222	17	Cordy	Kate	47	F	"	"	4015 Clifton roll
3225	223	18	Raach	Jesse	29	M	"	"	4214	"
3226	224	19	Chambers	Henry	26	M	"	"		
3227	225	20	Thompson	Lucinda	20	F	"	"	4217	"
3228	226	21	"	Daniel	22	M	"	"	4216	"
3229	227	22	Ross	Thomas	9	M	"	"	4218 Padockalı Cordy
3230	243	23	Daniels	Frank	29	M	"	"		
3231	244	24	"	Wm.	9	M	"	"	see that he is not the same as 2352
3232	303	25	Catin	Nettie	23	F	Saline Dist	3060 Clifton roll
3233	315	26	Field	Wm H	31	M	Illinois Dist	2668 Clifton
3234	316	27	"	Elias	10	M	"	"	2669	"
3235	318	29	French	Amanda	19	F	Cooweeskoowee Dist			

Cherokee Freedmen

Cher. No.	Miller No.	Dist. No.	Names		Age	Sex	Residence	
3236	320	30	Foster	Sarah	24	F	Cooweescoowee Dist	Formerly Snicker
3237	323	31	French	Charlotte	31	F	" "	Formerly Markham
3238	343	32	Ford	Rhoda	21	F	Illinois Dist	2647 Clifton roll
3239	360	33	Grimmett	Peggy	23	F	Cooweescoowee Dist	3471 Formerly Starr "
3240	364	34	Gunter	Phillis	45	F	" "	
3241	365	35	Groomer	Della	20	F	" "	2509 Clifton roll
3242	507	40	Leak	Elizabeth	27	F	" "	4243 1
3243	515	41	Looney	Josie	30	F	" "	4205 " Daughter of Jane Martin
3244	518	42	Lyons	Ned	19	M	" "	2835 Clifton roll
3245	519	43	"	Rachel	14	F	" "	2837 "
3246	520	44	"	Elias	22	M	" "	2836 "
3247			Irons	Winnie	20	F	" "	Bennetts Av. 28
3248	579	45	Martin	Mike	25	M	" "	2895 Clifton roll
3249	581	46	Martin	Mary C.	19	F	Delaware Dist	
3250	588	47	Mayes	Cynthia	15	F	Cooweescoowee Dist	4211 "
3251	642	51	Markham	Charlotte	19	F	" "	

88 No.	89	9 Dist	Names		age	44	Residence	
3252	644 Admitted list	52	McNair	Jennie	50	F	Cooweescoowee Dist	3000 Clifton
3253	678 Rejected list		McIntosh	Bettie	25	F	" "	3001 Clifton roll Bennetts p. 36
3254	649 Admitted list	53	McNair	Elmore	16	M	" "	3007 Clifton roll Pt. Jennie McNair
3255	653	54	Martin	John	25	M	" "	
3256	656	55	Meigs	Florence	25	F	" "	3064 Clifton roll Formerly Murrell
3257	659	57	Mayfield	Maggie	36	F	" "	3026 Clifton roll
3258	660	58	Thompson	Cornelius	16	M	" "	3027 "
3259	661	59	Mayfield	Emma	13	F	" "	2899 Clifton roll
3260	662	60	"	Malinda	11	F	" "	2900 "
3261	663	61	"	Nancy	9	F	" "	
3262	679	62	Martin	Israel	20	M	" "	2894 Clifton roll
3263	680	63	"	Lizzie	26	F	" "	
3264	683	64	Martin	Mary Ann	27	F	" "	4203 " See that she is not the same no 2671
3265	684	65	Peterson	Louvina	13	F	" "	4207 Clifton roll
3266	685	66	"	Charity	10	F	" "	4208
3267	735 Rejected		Martin	David	54	M	" "	4200 Clifton roll
3268	736		"	Wm H	18	M	" "	4206 "
3269			"	Eliza	19	F	" "	4204 "
3270	692	67	Mayes	Henry	34	M	" "	
3271	703	69	Musgrove	Wm	25	M	" "	3754 Clifton roll
3272	710	71	Morgan	Mary	25	F	Saline Dist	Deceased

Cherokee Freedmen

Off. No.	Weller roll 21	O. list 21	Names		age	Sex	Residence	
3273	738	73	Martin	Samuel	22	M	Cooweescoowee Dist	2864 Clifton
3274	761	77	McNair	Mary	27	F	" "	4233 "
3275	769	80	Nash	John	24	M	" "	
3276	784	81	Nave	Maria	66	F	Saline Dist	3834 "
3277	820	82	Rogers	Aggie	32	F	Cooweescoowee Dist	
3278	821	83	Nave	Susan	12	F	" "	
3279	822	84	"	Amanda	16	F	" "	
3280	823	85	Rogers	Mary	23	F	" "	3207 Clifton roll See that this is ont No 227
3281	851	87	Rector	Wm.	30	M	" "	
3282	852	88	"	Anna	25	F	" "	Formerly Thompson
3283	853	89	Ratcliffe	Eda	27	F	" "	3195 Clifton roll Formerly Schrimsher
3284	854	90	Ratcliffe	Eliza	72	F	" "	See No 1734 See letter to Moses Whitmire Dec 30, '91
3285	961	96	Smith	Eliza	37	F	" "	
3286	972	97	Starr	Malinda	33	F	" "	Give Ans 6 '91 Jd Geo. Starr husb. & adm
3287	1041	103	Todd	Rachel	16	F	" "	Formerly Martin
3288	1046	104	Bann	Isaac	16	M	" "	3219 Clifton roll
3289	1047	105	Whitmire	Jacob	14	M	" "	5576 Clifton roll
290			"	Albert	8	M	" "	2515 Bennett No 69. Born Janry 1883

Cherokee Freedmen

No.	Admitted Roll No.	Dist. No.	Names		age	Sex	Residence	
3291	1069	106	Vann	Charles	25	M	Cooweescoowee Dist	1876 Clifton roll
3292	1084	107	Vann	Eliza	25	F	" "	" "
3293	1089	108	Vann	Benjamin	23	M	Illinois Dist.	
3294	1096	109	Whitmire	Patsey	20	F	Cooweescoowee Dist	
3295	1098	111	Ward	George	24	M	" "	
3296	1137	113	Whitmire	Jane	27	F	" "	
3297	1141	114	Wolf	Grant	22	M	" "	4112
3298	1142	115	"	Fliny	21	F	" "	3447 "
3299	1161	118	Whitmire	Kate	31	F	" "	
3300	1168	119	Whitmire	Lydia	30	F	" "	3498 " Formerly Webber
3301	1179	120	Webber	Margaret	56	F	" "	4299 Clifton Roll
3302			Still	Eliza	39	F	" "	Bennett No. 81
3302			Manley	Kate	23	F	" "	Bennett No. 82
3304	1196	121	Vatie	Ophelia J.	28	F	" "	
3305	1212	123	Ward	Mary	45	F	" "	fd admis. Dist May 29, 91

Cherokee Freedmen

Off. No.	Dawes No.	D. List	Names		age	sex	Residence	
3306	1215	124	Ward	Emanuel	24	M	Cooweescoowee Dist 53 or	Clifton wall
3307	1216	125	Ward	Maria	25	F	" "	Deceased
3308	1227	127	Ward	Caroline	50	F	" "	
3309	1236	128	Ward	Louisa	64	F	" "	
3310		130	Vann	Emma	36	F	" "	
3311			Buffington	Rector		M	" "	Died Jan 14.91
3312			"	Maria	70	F	" "	
3313			"	Wm H.	41	M	" "	
3314			"	Georgiana	35	F	" "	
3315			"	Reuben	30	M	" "	
3316			Unwod	Mary	50	F	" "	3170 Clifton wall Formerly Markham
3317			"	Arthur	11	M	" "	3171 Clifton wall See R 20995 (91)
3318	755	75	Rogers	Cloe	15	F	" "	

Department of the Interior
Office Indian Affairs
June 25. 1891

The foregoing supplemental Schedule of Cherokee freedmen containing one hundred and two names comprising the names of 87 Cherokee freedmen, who were "admitted" by Special Agent Wallace as entitled to share with the Delawares and Shawnees in the per capita distribution of the sum of seventy-five thousand dollars, appropriated by the Act of Congress approved October 19, 1888 (25 Stats, p. 609) but by reason of the lack of sufficient evidence, in the opinion of this Office, were placed on a "Questioned List" for further proof to establish their claim to enrollment under the 9th Article of the Cherokee treaty of 1866, as entitled to participate in said fund; the names of ten individual claimants who filed their applications in this Office, with proofs in each case, as well as the five cases, not on said "Questioned List," but found by Agent Bennett to be entitled to enrollment; are herewith submitted; the proof required to establish their claims having been furnished and Agent Bennett being satisfied that the parties reported are entitled to participate in the distribution of said fund, with the recommendation that said schedule be approved by you, and that a per capita payment of fifteen dollars and fifty cents be made to each of said 102 claimants, that being the sum to which each is entitled to receive under the law.

J. J. Morgan
Commissioner

Department of the Interior, July 7th 1891
The foregoing Schedule of 102 names from page 172 to 178 is hereby approved
George Chandler
Acting Secretary

As recommended
Copy sent to agent Bennett July 11, 1891

2ⁿᵈ Supplemental Schedule of names of Cherokee Freedmen made by Leo E. Bennett, U.S. Indian Agent and reported by him February 6. & June 6. 1892, as entitled to share with the Delawares and Shawnees in the per capita distribution of the sum of $75.000, appropriated by the Act of Congress approved October 19. 1888 (25 Stats, p 609) and revised under the supervision of this Office.

Cherokee Freedmen

Office No.	Dawes Roll No.	Regular No.	Names				Residence	Remarks
3319		1	Adair	Rachel	35	F		alias Rachel Steele. See Phillips ad-mitted list no 63-66
3320		7	Alberty	Amanda	21	F		See that she is not the same as No 1193
3321		8	Alberty	Charlotte	14	F		
3322		9	Allen	Annie	22	F		Daughter of 3313 nee Buffington
3323	son of 1524	10	Alberty	John	10	M		Son of 1512 See that he is not the same as 1194
3324		11	Armstrong	Wiley	36	F		alias "Annie" Armstrong
3325		12	"	Mamie	18	F		
3326		13	"	John	11	M		
3327		14	Buffington	William	20	M		See that he is not the same as No 3123
3328		15	"	Rosa	16	F		
3329		16	"	Reuben	14	M		Children of 3313
3330		"	"	John	12	M		
3331		17	"	Bessie	9	F		Born Nov 1882
3332	child of 665		Bacon	Lula	8	F		Died Oct 16, 1886. child of No 2675
3333		22	Bean	Joseph	27	M		Husband of No 1508 See that he is not the same as 2160
3334		23	Brewer	Fannie	10	F		Child of No 416. See that she is not the same as 1950
3335		24	Bean	Angeline	35	F		nee Martin nee Vann
3336		25	Vann	Lizzie	13	F		

Cherokee Freedmen

Office No	Dawes No	Bunnell No	Names		Age	Sex	Residence	Remarks
3337	26		Bell	Mary	47	F		3682 Clifton roll
3338	27	"		George	23	M		3683 "
3339	28	"		William	20	M		3684 "
3340	29	"		Lesley	20	M		3685 "
3341	30	"		Granville	18	M		
3342	31		Brown	Mahala	57	F		2848 Clifton roll
3343	32		Carter	Victina	35	F	Delaware Dist	Nee Thompson
3344	33		Chouteau	Rose	31	F	Cooweescoowee Dist	Nee Vann, See that she is not No 326 or 1210
3345	34		Downing	Mary Ellen	36	F		Nee Martin, wife of No 2339
3346	35		Daniels	Harry	40	M		Slave of Jos. Daniels
3347	36	"		Margaret	14	F		
3348	37	"		Ransom	12	M		
3349	38	"		Maggie D	10	F		
3350	39		Daniel	Mary	26	F		3478 clifton roll alias Meigs daughter of No 2699 See that she is not the same as No 10. p. 188
	Dup. 40		Daniel	Elizabeth	60	F		wife of Peter Meigs No 2699 Duplicated. See 2748
3351	41		Drew	Geo Washington	75	M		3239 Clifton roll
3352		"		Diana	60	F		3240 "
3353		"		Charles	20	M		Died in 1888
3354	43		Drew	Dora	11	F		Grand child of 41 above

Cherokee Freedmen

Office Ind. No.	Dawes No.	Cherokee No.	Names		age	Sex	Residence	Remarks
3355	46		Foster	Percy	38	M		Son of # 196 Clifton roll, 104
3356	46½		Freeman	George	26	M		Son of 2381 3017 "
3357	47		Grimmett	Rhoda	54	F		
3358	57		Hudson	Sarah		F		3545 Clifton roll. See that this is not 1109. See about Sarah
3359	52		Hardwick	Moses	59	M		2822 Clifton roll
3360	53		"	Eliza	31	F		2823 Now Lynch "
3361	54		"	Mary	28	F		2824 "
3362	55		"	Nelson	26	M		2825 "
3363	56		"	William	22	M		2826 "
3364	57		"	Cyrus	20	M		2827 "
3365	58		"	Sarah	18	F		2828 "
3366	59		"	Lewis	13	M		2829 "
3367			Lynch	Arthur	11	M	2832 Clifton roll Son of 3360	He paid in Mayes Dist, put age at 6 years while she make age 11. See that the child was born after Mar 3.63 See that he is not 82593
3368	60		Hare	Abaham	56	M		4357 Clifton roll
3369	61		Johnson	Israel	45	M		2604 Clifton roll
3370	62		"	Joseph	11	M		2605 "
3371	63		"	Minnie	9	F		See that he is not 752
3372	64		Johnson	Ozy	16	M		Son of # 752
3373	65		Johnson	Delilah	26	F		4311 Clifton roll
3374	66		Johnson	Loula	14	F		Daughter of # 756

Cherokee Freedmen

1880	Dawson No.	1881	Names		age	Sex	Residence	Remarks
3375		67	Jones	Bettie	35	F		3803 Clifton roll
3376		67½	"	Annie	22	F		2653 Clifton roll
3377	489	68	Kell	Katie	46	F		No 38 on Questioned list
3378		69	Landrum	Nicholas M.	37	M		3789 Clifton roll
3379		70	Lee	Polly	43	F		1817 Clifton roll Family Radcliffe
2543	Infts	70½	Leak	Simeon	9	M		Born Jan. 5. 1853. 3 mo. of No. 153 See 2543
3380		71	McNair	Chanie	40	F		2849 Clifton roll Wife of No. 2628
3381		72	Martin	Fred	24	M		4156 Son of 2726 "
3382		76	Muldrow	Lettie	23	F		
3383		77	Lynch	Martha	10	F		
3384		78	Martin	Carrie	16	F		watch this case closely. See that she is Granddaughter of 876 or daughter of 2685 her claim as No. 899
3385		79	Martin	Eliza	19	F		See that she is the daughter of Jerry & not of David Martin No. 869.
3386		80	Meigs	Fannie		F		nee Shorton Daughter of No. 2966
3387		81	"	Nathan	11	M		3164 Clifton roll
3388		82	Nelson	Zach	10	M		Son of No. 874. Born Dec 12. 1882
3389		82½	Nave	Philip	9	M		4461 Clifton roll Son of 2768 Born Nov. 24. 1882

Office No.	Wallace No.	Drennen No.	Names		age	sex	Residence	Remarks
3390		83	Ross	Viney	38	F		366 ⅔ Clifton roll alias Frye alias Farris
3391		84	Reynolds	Harrison	12	M	}	children of No 712
3392		85	"	Henry	10	M	}	
3393		91	Ross	Moses	34	M		See that he is not 1757 - 1826 or 1836
3394		92	Rowe	Hannah		F		alias Foreman nee Martin, wife of No 2393. See that she is not the same as 734
3395		93	Rider	Henry Jr.	29	M		
3396		95	Rowe	Ella	3	F		Died in 1884, daughter of No 1701
3397		95¼	Rogers	Florence	20	F	}	2549 Clifton roll
3398			"	Clyde	17	M	}	2550 children of 2866 "
3399			"	Edgy	12	M	}	2551
3400		95½	Ross	Jacob	71	M		4181 "
3401			"	Maria Jane	42	F		4187 "
3402			"	Moses	23	M		4183 "
3403			"	Rosanna	18	F		4185
3404			"	William	16	M		see that he is not 1249 "
3405			"	Emma	14	F		4188 "
3406			"	Ella	10	F		4186 See that she was born before Mar. 3. 1883
3407		96	Starr	Lizzie	26	F		3472 Clifton roll Daughter of No 2943
3408		97	Starr	Mattie	24	F		" " No 2943. See that she is not the same as 1299

Cherokee Freedmen

Miss. No.	Miller Roll	Cherokee No.	Names		Age	Sex	Residence	Remarks
3409	98		Starr	Hannah	22	F		
3410	100		Smith	James	32	M		3809 Clifton roll. See that he is not the same as No 3037
3411	107		Thompson	Jordan	16	M		Son of No 860 See that he is not the same No 901
3412	108		Towers	Annie	62	F		wife of No 3505 Clifton roll of 2960
3413	109		Timms	Elijah	49	M		
3414	110		Tucker	Lettie	56	F		wife of No 2953
3415	111		Vann	Katie	26	F		see that she is not the same as No 670
3416	112		Vann	John	16/10	M		Son of No 3026
3417	113		Vann	Samuel	30	M		
3418	114		"	Rachel	37	F		Daughter of No 2726 Family Martin
3419	115		"	Nettie	16	F		
3420	116		"	William	12	M		
3421	117		"	Henry	10	M		
3422	118		"	Bettie	9	F		See that she was born before Mar 3, 1883
3423	119		Vann	Dennis	39	M		
3424	120		Vann	Hannah	29	F		wife of No 3011, daughter of No 2086 Family Johnson. See that she is not the same as 1416
3425	121		Wright	Lewis	29	M		2583 Clifton roll

Office No.	Dawes No.	Roll No.	Names		age	sex	Residence	Remarks
3426		124	Webber	Mary Ann	18	F		alias Mary E. Webber
3427		125	Whitmire	Hannah	16	F		
3428		126	Willis	Emma	17	F		3519 Clifton roll. Daughter of 2546 See evidence Wholly rejected list #126 child claims 2546 to be the grandmother.
3429		127	Whitmire	Lucy alias Lucy Jane	14	F		Daughter of #426. See where Lucy Whitmire #427 died.
3430		128	Wright, alias Whitmire	Phillis	50	F		3546 Clifton roll wife of # 3108
3431		129	Whitmire	Eliza	47	F		3462 Clifton roll Now Stevens formerly Mayes See whether on list #397
3432		130	Whitmire	Catherine	35	F		3540 Clifton roll wife of # 3059. See that she is not the same as #3299
3433		132	Webber	Rachel	38	F		Now Henderson
3434		133	Henderson	Russell	21	M		
3435		134	"	Bertie	14	F		
3436	Rejected 67	Rejected 3	Alberty	James	60	M	Choctaw No., IT	3547 Clifton roll
3437	68		"	James Jr.	20	M		3549 "
3438	69		"	Alexander	18	M		3548 "
3439	70		"	Joanna	15	F		3550 "
3440	71		"	Willis Jane	14	F		3551 See that she is not same as #9
3441			Alberty	Josie	28	F		wife of #13 daughter of Looney Alder Choctaw roll #218 & Cow. list. She died prior to 1883

Cherokee Freedmen

No.			Names		age	Sex	Residence	Remarks
3442	73	6	Allen	Millie	47	F		4302 Clifton roll
3443			Thompson	Ophelia	29	F		4312 "
3444	74		Curl	Julius	23	M		4313 "
3445	75		"	Riley	22	M		4314 "
3446	57	8	Archer	Thomas	45	M		3582 Clifton roll
3447	58		"	William	19	M		3583 "
3448	59		"	Eli	16	M		3584 "
3449	60		"	Rosa	14	F		3585 "
3450		10	Beck	Mary	40	F		Formerly Meigs
3451			"	Geo. Mitchell	15	M		Died Sept 27, 1886
3452			"	Nancy Jane	6	F		" June 13, 1886
3453	394	38	Fields	Jackson	36	M		3464 Clifton roll
3454		42	Gibson	Emerilla		F		a "Free Negro" Freed by
3455	468	43	Gibson	James	34	M		
3456	467	44	"	Noah	15	M		
3457	470	45	"	Paul	14	M		
3458	471	46	"	Joy A.	12	F		
3459	472	47	"	Samantha	8	F		
3460		81	McPherson	John	43	M		
3461		82	Mayes	Susan	67	F		2494 Clifton roll wife of #2695
3462		88	Nave	Eliza	23	F		wife of #2068

Cherokee Freedmen

Mill No.	Dawson No.	R. No.	Names		Age	Sex	Residence	Remarks
3463	Rejected 120	Vann	Presnell Patience dr	28	F		Died April 14. 1865 on Cher. Authelist as 331 Gov. Dick
3464	admitted 135	Robinson & Rogers	Mary	45	F		wife of d 2833 nee Cochran has live in Creek Nation, since 1866?
3465	136	Rogers	Lydia	15	F		
3466	137	"	Edie	12	M		
3467	138	"	Dolly	10	F		Born Feby 27. 1865
3468		Still	Pauline	26	F	Gov. Dick, Layer 70	
3469	Rej 702	McNair	Rolly	30	M	Gov. Dick	

Department of the Interior
Office Indian Affairs
October 19th 1892

The foregoing second supplemental schedule of Cherokee Freedmen, containing one hundred and fifty one names of persons entitled to share with the Delawares and Shawnees, in the per capita distribution of the sum of seventy five thousand dollars, appropriated by the Act of Congress approved October 19, 1888. (25 stat. p.609), being names either filed in this Office or reported by Agent Leo E Bennett as entitled to enrollment, the proof required to establish their respective -- claims having been furnished that the parties herein reported are entitled to participate therein, is herewith submitted with the recommendation that it be approved by you and that a per capita payment of fifteen dollars and fifty cents be made to each of said one hundred and fifty one claimants, or their representatives, that being the sum to which each is entitled to receive under the law.

T. J. Morgan
Commissioner

Department of the Interior
October 29th 1892

The foregoing second supplemental schedule of one hundred and fifty one names, numbered from 3319 to 3469 both inclusive, from pages 180 to 189, is hereby approved as recommended

Cyrus Bussey
Acting Secretary.

Copy sent to Agent Bennett Nov 4. 1892   247/274

3rd Supplemental Schedule of names of Cherokee freedmen, made by Marcus D. Shelby Acting U.S. Indian Agent, and reported by him, July 14, 1893, as entitled to share with the Delawares and Shawnees in the per capita distribution of the sum of $75,000 appropriated by the Act of Congress, approved October 19, 1888, (25 Stats. p 609) and censed under the supervision of this office.

Office No. 10.	Wallace No.	Shelby No.	Names		age	Sex	Residence	Remarks
3470			Adair	Frances	47	F		
3471			"	Joseph	22	M		
3472			"	Harrison	18	M		children of John & Charlotte Adair
3473			Beck	Lizzie	11	F		child of #956
3474	58 admitted	6	Bell	George C	25	M		Questioned list no 3
3475	59	7	"	Emily	18	F		" " " 4
3476	60	8	"	Nancy Ann	16	F		" " " 5
3477	61	9	"	Arthur	11	M		" " " 6
3478		10	Williams	Lizzie	26	F		Died Feby 1892 See that she is # 1955 mr no 61 — 3369 Clifton roll
3479			Bean	Ailsey	27	F		wife of #2210
3480		19	Bryant	Lillie	11	F		Daughter of #269

Cherokee Freedmen

Office No.	Wallace No.	Wallace col.	Names		age	sex	Residence	Remarks
	Rejected	admitted						
3481	151	11	Blythe	Abbie	43	F		3885 Clifton roll
3482	155	12	"	Anna	27	F		3886 Now Anna Young alias Bronnon
3483		13	"	Alice	24	F		3887 Now Lynch
3484	94	14	"	Mary	22	F		3888 Clifton roll Now Lynch
3485	152	15	"	Edmund	18	M		3889 "
3486	153	16	"	Nancy	13	F		3890 "
3487	154	17	"	Minnie	11	F		3891 " Born in 1882
3488	Ill Dist 109	20	Goody	John	16	M		Son of # 1015, Died in 1885
3489	Ill Dist 114	21	Goody	Nancy	60	F		Died in 1886
3490	Ill Dist 89	24	Crapo	Peter	69	M		Died in 1889
3491	90	25	"	Grace	68	F		Died in 1888
3492		26	Daniels nee Vann	Frances	34	F		3914 Clifton roll child of # 1939 was that she is act # 1377 mar # 2018
3493	Can Dist 11	27	Drew	Lewis	27	M		Died March 1886
3494	Rejected 381	Rejected 39	Fry alias Davis	Solomon	17	M		} Children of 3390
3495	382	40	"	Bertha	15	F		
3496	383	41	"	Fred	12	M		
3497	Ill Dist admitted 493	28	Ford	Julia	23	F		Formerly Vann
3498			Vann	Bishop	11	M		Born April 4, 1882 } Children
3499			Vann	Clara	23	F		Died March 31, 1883 } of 1932
3500		33	Johnson	Cornelius	6	M		Son of # 734. Died in 1885
3501	Nashville admitted 468	34	Johnson	David	30	M		3641 Clifton roll See 37 questions list

Cherokee Freedmen

Nill No	Soll No on No	Nelly No	Names		age	sex	Residence	Remarks
3502		admitted 35	Johnson	James	13	M		Son of N? 1312
3503	Rejected 616	Rejected 70	Jones	George Ann	33	F		3957 ! Clifton roll child of N? 2412
3504		admitted 36	Landrum	George	13	M		445 Clifton roll Son of N? 142
3505		37	Lynch	John	31	M		2256 # Clifton roll Son of 619
3506	Solicited 73	38	Lynch	Katie	17	F		Died November 1883
3507	74	39	"	Joseph	13	M		Children of 863 Died Nov 1883
3508	75	40	"	Jesse	11	M		Died November 1883
3509		41	Mayfield	Martha	22	F		
3510		42	Mayfield	Mary	44	F		
3511		43	"	Nancy	20	F		
3512		44	"	Joseph	18	M		
3513		45	"	Willie	16	M		
3514		46	"	Nathan	15	M		
3515		47	"	Sezanna	12	F		
3516		48	"	John	10	M		See that he was born before May 3. 1883
3517	rejected by L 679		McDaniel	Jake	32	M		Was in Cherokee Nation 1864
3518	admitted 637	49	McNair	Hannah	35	F	See Questioned child N? 50	wife of N? 2656, Questioned N? 657
3519	619		McNair née Thomas	Ruth	23	F	" " " N? 49	3491 # Clifton roll child of 2966, wife of 2639
3520		89	Meadows	Florence	11	F		1955 # child of 1731, Ann April 1882

Cherokee Freedmen

Office No.	Dawes No.	Roll No.	Names		age	Sex	Residence	Remarks
3521	Rejected 88	McPherson	Lolu	20	F		
3522	89	"	John Jr.	18	M		Children of 4260. Father has a farm
3523	90	"	Mary	15	F		
3524	91	"	Johns or Joseph	11	M		See title was born before Mar 3, 1883
3525	98	Murrell	Bodeen	74	M		
3526	99	"	Henry	28	M		
3527	100	"	Ellen	24	F		
3528	101	"	John	22	M		
3529	102	"	Roselta	20	F		
3530	103	"	Lucinda	18	F		
3531	104	"	Georgie	14			Report sex when you pay
	admitted						
3532	54	Rogers	Sarah	57	F		3175 Clifton roll
3533	55	"	Ella	20	F		3176 "
3534	56	"	Billy or William	19	M		3177 "
3535	57	"	Nina	18	M?		3178 "
3536	58	"	Levi	17	M		3180 "
3537	59	"	William?	16	M		3182 "
3538	60	"	Ham	15	M		3181 "
	Rejected						
3539	110	Rider	Dora	13	F		4234 Children of Mary McNair # 3274
3540	111	"	Adaline	11	F		4235 Clifton Born August 1882
	admitted						
3541	61	Smith	Jeannetta	16	F		child of # 2043, Died Sept 9, 1889
3542	954 for will 62	Smith	Nancy	35	F		3448 Clifton roll wife of 2924
	Rejected						
3543	141	Stidham	Mary	11	F		Daughter of # 1300, Born Jany 12, 1882

Cherokee Freedmen

Office No.	Wallace Roll Cherokee etc.	Kern Roll No.	Names		Age	Sex	Residence	Remarks
3544		63	Steel	Fannie	17	F		Children of 3319 3374 Clifton roll
3545		64	"	Monen	15	?		Report age when you apply 3375 "
3546		65	"	Claude	13	M		3376 "
3547		66	"	Rosie	11	F		Born Dec. 10. 1882 3377 "
3548		67	Thompson	Nellie	110	F		Died in 1886 or 1887
3549			Thornton	Katie	48	F		3488 Clifton roll wife of 2966
3550		68	Vann	Caroline	13	F		Child of 3423
3551		69	Vann	Dinah	47	F		See that she is not the same as 340
3552		70	Bean	Janetta	20	F		
3553	Wallace rejected 1140	74	Vann	Isabel	58	F	4106 Clifton roll	See 3541. that is 17 but changed to 53 & now Adams, nee Adams cited back to 17
3554	1141	75	Adams	Ben	26	M		3913 Clifton roll Alias Vann see that it is not 363
3555	1142	76	"	Keaty	25	F		4105 Clifton roll Now Rogers
3556	1143	77	"	Martha	23	F		425-1 "
3557	1144	78	Vann	Ellen	14	F		See that she is not 5133
3558		79	Vann	James	41	M		3938 Clifton roll See that he is not 3250 nor 1377 nor 3191
3559		80	"	Alta Maria	13	F		3939 Clifton roll
3560		81	"	Mary Jane	13	F		3940 "
3561			Vann	William	95	M		See that he is not 3009
3562	Wallace rejected 377		Vann	Delilah	45	F		wife of 3022

Cherokee Freedmen

Office No.	Acting Chief No.	Names		age	Sex	Residence	Remarks
3563	83	Walker	Mary	22	F		child of #2513, Died April 1883
3564	84	"	Lillie	11	F		Died Oct. 1888
3565	85	"	David	11	M		Born Feb 1882
3566	86	Washington	George	45	M		3357 Clifton roll
3567	87	Webber	Davis	10	F?		child of #463, Died abut 1886
3568	88	Wilson	Harriet	30	F		child of #1291, Died April 1884

Department of the Interior
Office Indian Affairs
August 7th 1893

The foregoing third supplemental schedule of Cherokee freedmen containing ninety-nine names of persons entitled to share with the Delawares and Shawnees, in the per capita distribution of the sum of $75,000, appropriated by the Act of Congress, approved October 19 1888 (25 Stat. p 609), being names either filed in this Office, or reported by the U.S. Indian Agent at Union Agency, as entitled to enrollment, the proof required to establish their respective claims having been furnished that the parties herein reported are entitled to participate therein, is herewith submitted with the recommendation that it be approved by you, and that a per capita payment of fifteen dollars and fifty cents be made to each of said 99 claimants, or their representatives, that being the sum to which each is entitled to receive under the law.

D. M. Browning
Commissioner

Department of the Interior, Aug 9th 1893

The foregoing third supplemental schedule of ninety-nine names, numbered from 3470 to 3568 both inclusive, from pages 191 to 196, is hereby approved as recommended Wm H. Sims
Acting Secretary